Feel The Edges

Carlos Ramos

Published and distributed by Ventus Books

Printed in the United States of America

Cover Design: Deepak Kumar Singh

Manuscript Editor: Jennifer Collins

More info at: www.FeelTheEdges.com
(info@feeltheedges.com)

Library of Congress Cataloguing in Publication Data: A catalog record for this book is available from the Library of Congress.

1st Edition, December 2016

ISBN-10: 0692820043
ISBN-13: 978-0692820049 (Ventus Books)

CONTENTS

———

For my mother

PROLOGUE

What is life? I've often times asked myself this question. When I go backpacking into nature, I can sit at night for hours, just staring at the moon and the stars. I try to put it all together in my mind, how everything is supposed to work in unison, asking myself: what is the meaning of us being here? It's wonderful to think about the big picture, but it's hard to feel it in my heart. Hard to feel it in my heart because it's impossible to comprehend all of it.

When I listen to the famous philosopher Alan Watts, speak about his perception of the world, he sounds amazing, as if he knows so much about the inner workings of it all – but at the same time, I feel that he doesn't fully explain the big picture. At the end of the day, nobody will understand the world in its entirety, but I think that's how it's supposed to be. To have a sense of wonder and your own explanation of the world. That's what makes everyone so different: everyone has a different perception of it.

One of the main reasons I decided to write this book was that I wanted to leave something positive behind. Ever since I finished college and entered the "real world", I just felt somewhat lost. I had so many ideas and dreams when I was young, but as time passed by at work, I felt like my ideas and creativity were slowly disappearing. Sometimes I would wake up in the middle of the night with a tightness in my chest, wondering why I wasn't doing something outstanding, something positive for the world. I felt I was just working for money, but not really knowing why. Maybe because that's what society instills in you as you grow up, or maybe I just did it because that's just what you do after college.

All these feelings and questions, led me on a quest to find my purpose, but as time passed, I became even more frustrated because I felt that by now I should have known what to do – I felt as if I did not do enough. But enough what? Enough searching? Enough learning? Enough work?

I know there are millions of people in the world who struggle with finding their purpose. Everyone tells you to "just find your purpose" or " if you're passionate about your work, you won't see it as work". I heard and read all these phrases countless times, but I feel as though it is just something that people say which sounds good, and yet nobody has an explanation about how to go find it, beyond other phrases such as "follow your dreams" or "trust your gut". As I began my quest to find my purpose, I constantly asked myself, "What the hell does that mean???" and "is following my passion really the right way to go about it"?

I constantly searched for my purpose and as I struggled finding it, I prayed this grand idea would come to me. (As if a meteor would just come from the sky and strike me.). I waited and waited and waited, and there was no grand idea… just frustration. One day, I was standing on top of a mountain peak in Colorado, at 12,000 feet, sitting on the edge of the mountain and trying to motivate myself to ski down it. I was nervous and scared standing at the edge, figuring out the best route to take. I worried about avalanches and if I would remain in control as I skied down the steep mountain. As I jumped off the edge, I felt tense and uneasy, but as I started to ski down I become entranced in pure bliss. In that moment, nothing mattered – my mind and body were entirely in the present, I felt very connected to the world and my mind. As I skied down, I felt the cold chisel at my face and the wind beckoning in my ears. Time disappeared with my skis swallowed in powdered snow. I felt very alive. Once at the bottom of the mountain, as I stood there trying to catch my breath and in awe of what just happened It hit me! It's about finding the edges.

See, my interpretation of a "life purpose" was wrong. I was searching for some predetermined cosmic life purpose, as if it was already decided when I was born. Furthermore it was my mission in life to find it, as it would lead me to a happier, more fulfilled life. The thing is, if we look at our lives in simple terms and the aspects of life that connects us all, we can begin to see the bigger picture. All of us here on earth have a finite amount of time to live. During this time here, we tend to direct our actions and in general most of our lives to essentially be… happy, but the most important ones that bring us happiness and help society/life move forward, are those actions that our heart calls us upon and whether or not we choose to listen to it. We also do many trivial things during our lives that serve as fillers, but do not bring fulfillment to our lives. It then becomes a measure of which of these two actions we choose to do the most, which then correlates to our level of happiness and fulfillment. Once we know this, we can begin to understand what our life purpose really is and what we are supposed to do, to go about finding it.

I realized, that in order to find my purpose and essentially get to know myself and the world around me better, it wasn't going to involve me living my life running angrily in the world looking for some specific purpose or a predetermined thing that society puts in front us to seek and wishing that by some miracle I find it; instead I had to ask myself better questions, such as what is important to me? What edges should I be seeking? And what fulfills my heart? Which of these questions would serve as better guides, as to what I believed my purpose was. Then my journey began....

When I started writing this book and sharing my ideas, one of the most common questions I received was "What is wrong with living a perfectly content life? Why is it wrong to live a comfortable life? Why not just stay in the middle, avoiding the edges? Why not ski the greens, spending my afternoon in the bar, drinking hot chocolate by the fire? These are perfectly valid questions. In fact some of life's most difficult questions. It seems there are millions of people in the world who are perfectly fine living a life by the fire. The fire is ok. Are you happy with acceptable? Do you want average? Or do you want extraordinary? Remarkable? Live out your legacy with your natural born unique abilities? Do you ask those difficult questions? Who are we? Why are we here? What can I contribute to my friends, family, to society, to the world? If you ask these questions then I am writing to you. Keep reading. Let us discover our edges together and uncover these difficult questions that nature has instilled in us. A sense of wonder of who we are and what our heart is saying. Let's not allow society to drown these thoughts and desires. It is our duty to purposefully and intentionally seek the edges of life. The edges that bring us fulfillment, happiness and most importantly resonate with our heart.

My goal for this book is to light a passion in you to successfully navigate your life with more purpose and understanding. To be closer to living a life of purpose. To serve as a beacon for others that are lost and can't find the right paths to their edges. And lastly, to not only explore your edges, but to conquer them with confidence and excitement.

II.

One more thing before we go on.. and this applies to all aspects of your life – don't believe anything anyone says unless it agrees with your own reason, your own common sense, and your own heart. I want you to think about what I'm saying in relation to your life and find a common ground between my experiences and yours. If you can deeply identify with certain topics or stories, ask yourself why. And, how can you move closer to the edge of that part of your life? We are all different; we all have had different experiences in our lives that shaped the way we interpret the world around us. I want to leave that freedom and individuality you possess untouched –. My goal is to be able to reach your heart and make you feel it as best as you can. I want to get you closer to the edges, to awaken those feelings that have been suppressed by the world around us. I will talk about concepts that run our daily lives and how we can conceptually and mindfully feel the edges of them.

I'm not out to compete with any one, I'm here to complete, by encouraging and inspiring souls through a text at a time

-Bernard Kelvin Clive

There is no greater agony than bearing an untold story inside you.

-Maya Angelou

Part One-What is the Edge?

I want to stand as close to the edge as I can without going over.
Out on the edge you see all kinds of things you can't see from the center.
-Kurt Vonnegut

The Imago Mundi is a Babylonian map and is the oldest known world map. It dates back to around the turn of the 5th century. The map is carved in a clay tablet where it depicts the world as being a land completely surrounded by water; anything else occurring after the ocean were mythological objects or, as some like to depict it, the end of the world. For thousands of years, people believed the world was essentially flat and that it had an end. If you went too far, you would go over the edge. This "Edge" instilled fear in sailors and most would not dare to go there. Although this was a physical edge on a map, it represented more than that. This represented the Edge of discovery and one that some of their hearts called on them to seek.

Sometimes when I look out on the ocean, I wonder what is in the vast open water and what is beyond that horizon in which I cannot see past. This is the physical edge that many explorers have seen and which has ignited their individual fire to go to that Edge. Civilizations once thought that the world was flat. That you would go over the edge, until brave explorers decided to go against "rational thought" or "scientific facts" and see this edge for themselves. In essence, they pushed the boundary and were ready to go into uncharted waters for this Edge.

The Edge, to them, was the unknown – the missing piece of the puzzle that needed to be found. The engine for human evolution has been this missing piece, the unknown. The people in our world who have pushed the human envelope and catapulted our species to the next level were in search of the Edge, for the unknown. Isaac Newton needed to get to the edge of how gravity worked; Martin Luther King, Jr. found his Edge and made it his life's work to get society to feel that Edge, the Edge of equality. As the Babylonian map had a physical edge, in comparison to our lives, our edges no longer become physical, in turn become transcendental as relating to the human experience. As we live through our lives, we too have edges of many aspects of our lives and they can have many different meanings to us. It's something that constantly changes, but the core concept remains the same.

I believe that all of us are in a search for certain edges and sometimes we know it, but I am convinced that most of the time we don't understand it or realize it. Is this search, sparked/fueled by a basic instinctual drive or is it from understanding and following one's hearts? I believe it's a combination of both, but is one in which we can determine how close we get to those edges that fulfill our lives by being more aware of our hearts. You, reading this book right now, might be in a search for something, a missing piece of your puzzle. We have many different puzzles in our lives, but usually one tends to stick out, according to a particular moment in life.

Many of us are in a search for a specific edge which our heart calls us to, but a multitude of us just stop looking, not because we don't want to, but because the noise of society has made it hard to. We simply sit and let other distractions keep us busy, instead of finding our edges. Life becomes stagnant, dull tasting, with small glimpses of those edges, and yet we turn our backs on those edges; and as we get older, we walk further and further from them, until that missing piece of our puzzle is lost in time forever.

The further away we walk from that edge, the harder it is to find it, but the path back is always there for us to turn around on... so that you might head towards the edge.

Fire Safety

I remember, very vividly, backpacking through the Rocky Mountains and, at night before I went to sleep, I would take pictures of the night sky; but with the fire going, it was a bit hard to get a really good picture, let alone find something to focus on from afar and the light of the campfire. I didn't dare leave the warmth and protection the fire gave me at night. As the ranger had told me earlier, the place was home to mountain lions and coyotes, so that thought remained in my mind throughout the night. Being in a remote place with no one around me for miles, leaving the comfort of the fire was no option. Sitting there, though, I kept thinking: what was outside of this warmth and protection? What kind of picture could I get?

I looked at the darkness, then looked at the fire, then the darkness, fire, darkness, fire, darkness…. "Oh, what the hell," I said; I couldn't bare it anymore. I packed my gear and frightfully left camp, as well as the comfort of the fire. There was a high open area which I estimated to be about a half mile from camp. As I walked nervously, stopping to listen every few steps or so and looking back to see just the twinkle of the fire, anxiety started to take over. Every sound was a "what if?" But I kept going one foot after the other. The more I walked, the less anxiety I felt, but still I had an uneasy feeling in my body.

During the walk, I felt very alone and wondered if this is how people feel when they're going towards the unknown, but at the same time, my eyes started adjusting to the darkness and everything was becoming less frightening. Beauty started to come out. Nature is a very different place at night, one of the most peaceful and serene places on earth. No sounds except the trees swaying as the wind blows by. I finally got to the top of the hill, and found it overlooking a majestic lake. I felt like the only person in the world in that moment. I closed my eyes and I could hear the wind blowing by in waves that sounded just like real ocean waves passing by without the crash. Everything just seemed surreal. As I sat there overlooking the lake, I thought – "what if I just never left the comfort of the fire? I would have missed out on all this: this beauty, this feeling, and this lesson."

Everything in life has an edge, and I believe the core ones which drive us are love, fear, action, unity, and death. In the rest of this book, these edges will be broken down, with hopes of giving them a bit more meaning and understanding for you, to keep you feeling for them.

You see, many of us stay too far from the edge, or simply wonder away. Imagine for a second that you were blind and were standing on the top of the tallest waterfall in the world, and you were supposed to walk to the very edge. Your reward for walking towards the edge would be that, the closer you get to it, the more your vision would come back and be better able to see the beauty of the world around you. You hear the water roaring, the wind blowing in your face. Close your eyes for a moment and picture yourself there. How would you do it? Would you even do it? You see, many of us would be too scared to even start something like this small journey. You'd have to get on your knees and crawl with your hands in front of you as you felt the ground and all your surroundings, all with the possibility of getting hurt/falling over, and the unknown, until you felt the edge. This is why this journey is so important to embark on.

Childhood Dreams

Like the 5th century sailors were warned to be careful not to go too far or they would go over the edge, because at that time that part of the ocean was unknown to them. This early thinking was the basis for the manner in which society affects us today . Many of us are told to play it safe and stay away from unmarked paths, to not stray away from the pack, to always listen to those older than you and get good grades and go to college then get a good job, and that one's value is determined by how much money and expensive things we have. If we don't pay attention to the bigger picture, we can sometimes let society molds us into what it wants us to be and who we really are in our core is lost in time and our hearts are silenced.

This has been a recurring theme in many people's lives as they get older. I remember being around the age of six, and after school, I would walk to my mother's restaurant to wait for her to be done so that she would then take me home. I usually had to wait for a couple of hours around a bunch of cooks and servers, and with no one my age to play with, I would go "exploring" around the restaurant on my own in order to entertain myself and help pass the time.

My mother was crazy busy when she was running the restaurant, therefore didn't have time to watch over me while I waited for her.

On some occasions, I would just sit and watch the cooks at their craft; I was just sitting there patiently, in wonder as to what they were doing with each ingredient. I would sit and taste raisins, olives, shredded beef, vegetables, and different fruits, just taking my time with each one as I experienced these flavors for the first time. I was a small young Issac Newton in a sense, just playing with the world around me with no regard for what the meaning of each of my actions was, with no fear of judgment, no fear of disapproval, and no fear of whether something would work or not. I was being my natural human self, exploring the world around me.

I see this in kids many times. They are going to the Edge to see how close they can get to it. Children are tasting, touching everything, and constantly striving to feel the world around them, but then society steps in and says... 'NO! SIT HERE! ACT LIKE THIS! DON'T TOUCH THAT! SEEK THIS!

Some parents take all kinds of measures to "protect their kids" from feeling the edges. This is normal, as parents must guide their children in the world, but many parents are either too cautious or too extreme. They are pulling their children from the edges, which is reinforced as children start to be more and more exposed to society and eventually enter school. This is what many kids experience growing up. They first start experimenting with the world around them as they follow their heart, but the noise of society often times starts to interrupt their hearts.

Hiking Trails

When backpacking, you sometimes hit parts of the trail where they diverge and each trail goes a different way, with a different experience attached. Some trails are more treacherous than others, some have more beauty than others, and some lead you to undiscovered places. Life is full of these same crossroads as we move through it. Many people get stuck in these crossroads, not knowing where to go; they sit and wait, hoping someone will pass by and direct them on the right path. Some people choose paths based on how easy they are or which one will be the most rewarding. In order to reach the edges, you must choose the paths that give you fear since, most of the time, the path to the edge is the scary one.

During a backpacking trip I experienced, there was a very popular waterfall that one could access by car. There are bathrooms there, a snack bar, and a drinking fountain. There's another way to access it also, and that's by foot. It's a two day long hike to get to it, with many steep rocky climbs and many unmarked paths. My friend Mike and I, being twenty two years old at that time and wanting to test out our manly woodmen selves, having grown up in a city, decided to take the path less traveled. Excited for our adventure, we set out on an early Friday morning. As we walked into the forest, I remember looking back at the car and feeling a bit of anxiety, and I briefly asked myself, 'Why didn't we just drive to this thing?' During most of the day, we walked, crossing rivers, going up and down hills. Mike and I talked a lot during that hike. I got to learn stuff about him that I'd never known, even after knowing him for several years. I got to see a different side of my friend, one that most people are too fearful to show. Most of our conversations before had only really involved sports, girls, and parties. This time was different, though I'm not sure if it was just being bored and being forced to talk, but I learned a lot about Mike. His dreams, his past... and I got a glimpse of who he was as a person, this insight into his core is something that can never be bought.

As it got late that first day, we decided it was time to set up camp. Since it was our first real adventure out in the wilderness, we decided we had to find the perfect camping spot. As we walked, we found some awesome places... next to a river, underneath a canopy of trees, but it wasn't enough, and so we kept walking; we wanted to find the perfect one. Finally, as we walked, we heard a loud roaring sound. "It's a waterfall!" We both yelled. We ran towards it and, after going through some trees, we came up to this huge waterfall. Man, was it beautiful. I had never seen anything like that. As we sat there in awe, really taking everything in – the mist, the sound, the open view – we lost track of time and realized we had to quickly start setting up camp, as it was getting dark. By the time we set up our tents, it was already dark and we still had to gather wood... We ventured out at night, looking for wood, which felt very uncomfortable as it was eerily quiet and dark. We had never backpacked into the woods that far. During that search, we ran into an old narrow wooden bridge. What was great about this bridge, was that it gave you a complete view of the sky. We headed back to camp after gathering wood. After eating some pre-packaged soup and rice, we both poured some apple cinnamon moonshine to sip since it was starting to get pretty cold; and then we decided to head out to that bridge to see the night time sky.

Man! When we got to the bridge and our eyes adjusted, the night sky just lit up. I had never seen the stars in that way. You could see the white contrast of the Milky Way band perfectly... Orion's Belt, the Big and Little Dipper, Hercules, Sagitarius... you name it, it was there. Sitting on that bridge and looking up at the stars made me think about my life and the grand scheme of all things. I like to think that, during that night, my view of the world changed a bit in the sense that I felt that life is more connected than we might think. It's odd to look at the universe and really feel part of it, but looking at the night sky that night made me feel it.

The next day was not so grandiose. We both got up, ate an energy bar, and headed out since we knew a lot of uncovered terrain was still left. The previous day had been cloudy and much cooler, but this day was the complete opposite. Less tree cover, not a cloud in the sky, hot, and many more steep rocky climbs. With no sunscreen, we were both being scorched by the sun, the packs on our backs starting to feel heavier as we climbed. We both ran out of water with no stream in sight, which made it even more miserable. There was very little talking, as we both just wanted to get to the waterfall and go home at that point. My lips were chapped, face sunburned, and I had only one thought in my mind – the Gatorade I'd left in the car. At about mid-afternoon, we were walking along a path, and in the distance I could see a kid eating cotton candy; I seriously thought I was seeing a mirage for a moment, but as we got closer, I could see the kid, and then saw another person with a stroller.

WE'RE HERE! I remember walking to the ledge of the waterfall and seeing so many tourist people there, with their hats and water bottles in their hands. People looked at us a bit weird, not realizing we had just walked two days to get there. Sitting there, I thought: 'When I have a child, I will take him with me on the backpacking trip', because that trip was filled with so many different experiences and beauty. I saw so much that I had never seen before during those two days as compared to what I would have seen if I just drove to the final point. I cherished and enjoyed that waterfall so much more because my journey was different. The waterfall was a place; the journey there got me closer to the edges. Walking towards the edge, there was so much more to experience, so much more to appreciate.

That's what we're losing in our society, the need to walk along those edges. Sometimes, we reach an edge without realizing it, but most of the time, we have to constantly be aware of ourselves and push toward finding those edges in our lives. The Edge is the place that most people fear to go to, as the comfort of the inside – "the norm" – is much easier to stay at, instead of wandering out in the unknown to find surprises, and even change, in how we view the world. You might ask, but why is it important that I seek the edge? What if I'm perfectly fine in the middle?

I believe we are all searching for some edge in our lives even though it could be good or bad. I believe it's either societal/ego driven or one that our hearts calls us on and the way our life plays out is determined by which edges we seek. Such as love, hate, fear, greed, laziness, and productivity. What I'm trying to convey in this book is to give you a perspective of what I believe is a core driver in our lives (edges we seek) and if we understand this and focus on the ones that truly speak to our hearts, they can make a huge impact in our lives.

Many of us resist change, but we must constantly defy the norms, the middle, and go to the outside to find a hidden talent, perspective, or priceless love. In the next parts of this book, I will tell you about some of those edges that are the biggest players in our lives, and what I've done in my life to get closer to them.

Part Two- Love: The Fuel for Everything

"Only True Love, can fuel the hard work that awaits you"
-Tom Freston

Have you ever asked the question – what is love, and what does it do? Love, is the substance that gives life true meaning. Love is the Carbon to every life that has ever existed on earth. Love is the game changer in the game of life.

If we reflect on why we do most things in life, for many of us the search for love is at the forefront. Most people want to be successful, liked, wanted, desired, hugged, kissed, fed, talked to, and to feel safe, feel warm, feel loved…. These are some of the main drivers to everything we do in life. There are those who have all the riches in the world, but still are in search for their heart. Now you might ask, What about those that commit evil in the world? Are they coming from a place of love? I believe that at the core we are doing it for the need of love. Take for example, someone who has been treated terribly by society and they have endured much turmoil in their life. They might be so angry at the world for not fulfilling that need for love, that they are angry towards the world around them. They treat others badly and their disregard for other's lives often times diminishes, but at the core the reason is this unfulfilled love we all as humans seek. Mahatma Ghandi once said "hate the sin, love the sinner". He says love the sinner, because deep down that is what the sinner is seeking and by loving them less more sin occurs.

We are greedy for love, we are sad for love, we are happy for love, we cry for love, we fight for love, we argue for love, we work for love, we eat for love, we play for love, we sing for love, and we dream for love. Love is the central part of all creation.

We were put on earth to love. We make it so hard on ourselves on a daily basis, thinking about what to do, what the meaning of life is, and I believe it is to love.

Love is a fuel, a power that we must harness every day of our lives. If used correctly, it can make you a very powerful being. The world will serve those who love.

Instruments of The Universe

Love is something that we are born with, but often times as we get older and the love is hard to feel, we suppress the need for it and focus that energy on the things that society says will get us closer to love. Which in turn lead us to walk further and further away from the edges of love. We concentrate on our survival, jobs, bank accounts, the cars we drive, the houses we live in, and all this noise starts to blur our perceptions of love. We start to see ourselves as ordinary beings, and we lose the big picture of the universe and the role that we play in it. Yes…. You do play a very important role, a vital role in the grand scheme of things. Most of us don't realize the parts that we are supposed to play. We get caught up in the material things, in search of finding love. Many of us think that if we obtain importance, money, and expensive things, this will make it easier to find love, and it becomes a never-ending cycle.

For some of us the cycle might start by seeing the journey of college as being one that is vital so we can get a great paying job and make a great deal of money, so we can have a nice house, sports cars, and a great family. It's not wrong to think about having nice things, but the problem comes when you think having a certain bank account value is going to give you love, because it usually lets people down at the end of their lives. I remember many times when I would have a hard time falling asleep, thinking about work, feeling anxiety because I felt I wasn't where I wanted to be. I didn't have the amount of money I wanted to have in my bank account. I felt ashamed that I was not doing something big – I did not own a house yet, I still had debt I was paying off and I was working a job which did not fulfill me. I felt inadequate as a Human being. I was nervously running through my life in search for the wrong things. Like Mahatma

Ghandi once said "A very slow movement on the right way is better than overwhelming speed on the wrong path". I was hastily looking for love, but I was going about it the wrong way.

We must realize that love starts with us. Regardless of how you believe life started, imagine that it started with what science says today. Something started this universe, whether it was the supreme creator or the big bang: something created all of this in perfection. How is this beauty going to be translated/experienced? How is it going to be seen? How is it going to be felt? How is it going to be heard? How is it going to be smelled?

This is why we are here. This is why love was created. Love is the translation of all this beauty in the world, Love is the Rosetta Stone of the world around us. It is through this that the world around us is truly felt. And, if love is the Rosetta Stone, then we are the translators. Through our vision, sight, smell, taste, touch, and mind, we are able to serve as the medium between love and the world. We are the connectors: without sight, humanity could not see the beauty of an ocean view. Without the ability to hear, we could not listen to the sound of music created around us, and without taste, we could not taste the sweetness of the tart yet sweet taste of a mango. Without the ability to smell, we would not be able to smell the rain. Without the ability to touch, we would not be able to feel our loved ones' warmth. Without our minds, we would not be able to freely interpret the world around us. Without these abilities, we would be trapped in a dark and lonely space.

You could be walking in a field of wildflowers and have no idea; there would be no smiles, no expression, no wonder, no appreciation for the greatness of the earth's existence. In essence, there would be no meaning, no translator of the beauty that is our world. Love, therefore, is the chemical agent that gives life to life. Now I'm not saying that everyone sees the world through rose-colored lenses as we all at times experience hardship and pain which makes it difficult to see the beauty that is around us, but what I mean is that love is always there even in the most difficult of times and it is up to us to choose to acknowledge it.

Love is the stimulant that gets life moving. Beauty is instilled in all of us, by the world that amazed us from the moment we were born. Love makes us enthusiastic, Love makes us care about each other, about animals, about our environment, about the world that has been created. It is nature/the creator's insurance policy on a masterpiece, our world.

What Does Love Do for Me?

As I started writing this book, I knew there was going to be a time where I had to decide which edge I felt was the most important. I constantly found myself in conflict as to which edge I was going to start writing about. I knew I had to start with the most fundamental, the Edge that we must seek first before we seek others. To me, the first Edge is the one where, if you constantly seek, it will get you to where you want to be and it is going to hold you through life most of the way. It will constantly give your life meaning, whether you are rich or poor. It will not steer you wrong. It's going to take you through some twists and turns, and sometimes dark places, but it will get you to the light. It is going to give you fuel to always keep moving in the right direction, guided by your heart.

What has love meant to you in the past? This is one of the edges we must constantly be aware of. Who or what do you love, and why? These are two questions we must ask ourselves constantly. Ask yourself 'why?' When you need guidance. Ask yourself 'who?' when you need strength. This is the one edge which many of us put last, and the rest of our lives are houses with no foundations. It's very hard to go through the world without this edge, regardless of whether you have all the money in the world. This Edge can't be bought, this Edge is priceless, and this Edge is only learned and experienced.

Just like the universe needs us to experience the world, we need love to experience the world itself. That's what love does for you. It lets you experience every single beauty the world has. It gives you permission to feel the love for someone when you're young and you haven't even learned much about the world. To feel the love from your son or daughter, to feel the love from your friends, to fall in

21

love for your passion, to allow you to work and run towards your dreams when everyone else thinks you're crazy.

During the times that you were alone, chasing your dream, love has stood next to you, giving you pep talks along the way. It is your cheerleader when no one else is cheering. It is what makes people do extraordinary acts of kindness. It is what makes people do courageous things. Love rewards us with these experiences, and it is the biggest reward we can get, by always moving closer to the Edge of love.

Seeking Love Blindly

You ever hear people say, "he or she is just blinded by love"? Are we wrong or stupid for being blinded by love? Is this the right way to seek the Edge of love? I've asked myself these questions before, especially in times of what I like to call hard love. Where you feel this extreme and passionate love despite moments of hardship. Whether seeking your dream or fighting for someone you love, there are moments when everyone is telling you to turn back, to let them go, that your idea won't work, that it will never happen, that you will never find them, to throw in the towel, to turn in your keys, and quit…. Love finds ways to blind you, so that you don't pay attention to these things. It is your coach. It is telling you to keep pushing, to keep fighting, and you somehow push through. You find your dream, find your love or get your love back, or obtain that life that you desire to live.

Just like in the search of love, we get our hearts broken; we must constantly push, knowing that heartbreaks are just part of the whole journey and we must acknowledge this fact. This is the barrier that people don't like to cross, this is the part of the journey that scares most people. "What if I get my get my hopes up? What if I get my heart broken?" This is part of the journey, the bumps in the road, but as long as we keep moving closer to the Edge of love, we will live a more meaningful life.

You must go into this journey, ready and willing to stand as close to the Edge as you can. You must let go of all inhibitions, all fears; you must trust that – as long as you are seeking love – it is going to get you closer. There are times when love blinds you and you end up getting your spouse back, your company becomes successful, your startup goes big, you find your dream job, you find your love again, you change the world for the better, or you stand up for injustice when no one else does. Your one gesture can cause a huge ripple and change the world. Love will sometimes blind you, for what you seek is important in your heart. This is why we must accept this fact of life, that sometimes it will blind you in the quest for love, but most of the time, it blinds you so that you actually follow your heart and not what others are telling you.

Many times in my life, I've felt an indescribable feeling of passion, fire-burning that has given me the ability to feel things I thought one could never feel, and the love that – when you see that person who means the most to you – your world just becomes meaningful.

Once you experience innocent, clean love, where you are in pure bliss, it becomes your edge. You've now reached a new edge, so you have been enlightened in a way. Now that you see where that specific edge is, you will then know: that edge is permanently there as a symbol of guidance that you can always use to go back to in moments when you feel you are lost or backtracking on your quest for the Edge of love. It becomes your beacon. Once you've reached that feeling of love, you must continue to push to get as close to the edge as you can.

Keep searching for the thing you love to do, keep working toward that dream, keep fighting for those you love, keep standing up for injustice, and always keep pushing to feel closer to love.

In The Dark

There will be moments in our lives when we feel that love is not there. "Where did it go? How come I felt so much love before, and now I feel none?" These are some questions that from time to time I've asked myself. These have been dark times in my life. One instance I remember sitting in my office and feeling lost, aimlessly clicking between my email account and social media, having no purpose; in these moments, I knew I was walking away from the Edge of love. I know the feeling, I can feel it in my heart when I'm walking away from love. It is a feeling of your mind letting you know that you have given up, that you are choosing to go the opposite way.

When this happens, indifference and hate have a funny way of replacing that edge. Instead of heading towards love, you all of a sudden start heading towards the darkness, that place where everything is dark, cold, and meaningless. Everything is against you, nothing goes your way, and you start to lose yourself. You are now walking towards this edge. At first, you become indifferent. You become lost in the banality of the day to day, things lose their color, food loses its taste, and you can no longer smell the proverbial flowers. Your senses become dull, and things no longer excite you. We feel alone and fragile, but we are emotional creatures, and something has to start replacing those emotions of love. We can't just remain indifferent; we start to become irritated by the world around us. The world starts to become something that we must fight with on an everyday basis, just to get through the day.

We get frustrated with the person driving too slowly in front of us. Music becomes an annoyance. Happy and energetic people become irritating to be around. The barista doesn't spell your name correctly and it ruins the rest of your day. We simply slowly begin to shut down all the beauty and love that is around us. Hate and indifference start to cloud the light of love in our hearts.

Society has made it a taboo to talk about our bad feelings with one another. We are all supposed to be joyful and happy. Let's face it, though: we all have experienced these moments of turmoil in our lives. Times where we feel lost and cold. It's essential though to know these feelings before we can truly begin to move closer to the Edge of love. South cannot exist without the North, light cannot exist without dark; we have to experience these moments of sadness as part of our emotional compass. Sometimes in our lives, we have to be in darkness in order to be able to see where the light is. This has been proven in history, time and time again.

I was fortunate to have someone in my life who taught me about being in the darkness, and how it helps you see the light. My paternal grandfather was left without a father when his father abandoned him and his mother when he was young. This was a time when women generally depended greatly on the men in their lives because women had very few rights. My grandparents were poor, literally dirt poor. My grandpa and his mother lived in a shack, with dirt floors and a roof made out of tin sheets. He worked as a mule handler, taking care of the mules and cleaning their stables. At the end of each night, he would get his dinner which consisted of milk and some bread. Each night, he would come home and share his dinner with his mother.

I remember him telling me that it was one of the worst periods of his life. He told me that seeing his mother in such terrible condition each night broke his heart. He felt alone, helpless, afraid, and many times, he would cry by himself on the way home at night. He was in the dark; he was in survival mode and it was him against the world. I asked him, 'where was the light for you?' He said, "the bread and my mother". "My mother's love kept me going in a world full of darkness, and the bread was my way out." He hated the taste of the bread; he would eat the same bread each night and often times he would think of what flavors he would add to make the bread taste better. He made it his purpose to create a better bread and come out of his circumstances, but did not know how he was going to do it since he didn't have much money saved up.

His boss' son had started a bakery, but was struggling and needed help. He asked his boss if he could work there half the time instead in order to help his son out. He ended up working there full time, and became a full time assistant baker. After about a year, the son did not want to run the bakery any longer – he wanted out. This was where my grandpa started to realize that the light was getting brighter, and he offered to buy the bakery. With the profits, he would pay him back the rest of the money. The man agreed and my grandpa started running his own bakery. He knew he had to do something different to make his bakery stand out. He remembered about the flavors! He started by adding rosemary and rye to the bread, as he loved the smell of rosemary and the taste of rye. It became his best seller. He and his mother moved to the bakery and had a much better living. After a couple years of his successful bakery business, he opened the first movie theater in his town, and shortly after started an orange grove. During the dark times, he'd been able to see the light in the far distance, but just had to keep walking towards it to reach it.

We all have to experience these moments in order to see where the light truly is; the decision maker in all of this is whether you are going to sit still or start walking towards the light. Many of us know what we should do, but first we need to seek love as our source of strength.

Finding The One

Most of the core drivers in our lives, whether we realize it or not, have a general purpose. We clean our cars before a date, to give a better impression, we go to the gym to stay in shape, and many of our everyday habits can somehow lead to our purpose. We are intelligent creatures; our conscious and subconscious mind are constantly analyzing everything that happens around us. Like Maxwell Maltz says in the book *Psychocybernetics*, that our brains are like giant super computers, and a physical form of it can never be built to simulate the processing power our brains have.

Most of the time, we go through our day, undertaking basic tasks, thinking about certain things, but do you ever think, what is the actual source that leads you to make these decisions? See, we are logical creatures, most of the time.… Things have to somehow make sense to us in order for us to proceed with the action followed. What action? The action that you are planning on; for example moving to another state, applying for another job, going to school to seek a new career, running marathons to become more physically fit, or starting your own business to become wealthy. These are all actions we take on our lives, but if you really trace them back in detail, they each lead to a specific source, a specific reason why we are taking that action.

Maybe you are moving to another state to seek a new beginning, but maybe you're really running from your past. You're applying for another job because you want to make more money, but maybe you're just trying to keep up with the joneses, or you're going to school to seek a new career because you're tired of your old one, but maybe you just miss learning and, somehow deep inside, you yearn for higher level knowledge. You're running marathons to become fit and feel healthier, but maybe you're running fiercely as a way to cope with a loved one's passing. Maybe you're starting that new business not to specifically become wealthy, but because you no longer see your children as a result of being overworked by your current job and would like more time freedom to be able to spend with your family.

Understanding the core of why we pursue certain actions is the secret to unraveling who we really are – this understanding will push you along in times of hardship and confusion, and tell you why you are doing it. Many of the things we do in life somehow tie back to love. Often times for those who are greedy and never feel they have enough power or wealth, somehow, they tend to think that the more money they have, the more they will be liked, despite the actual fact that you shouldn't expect people to truly love you because you have money. Many people in this state are not necessarily addicted to power and money, but they are searching/craving for genuine love.

Just like every human being, you need love to truly thrive. I don't care who you are; we are all creatures of love. I am certain of this, that even the man who's sitting alone in his island mansion with all the riches in the world is staring at the vast ocean, hoping somebody comes by knocking. The mother who is working, cleaning hotel rooms and leaving her children alone at home, is thinking about them as she works overtime so she can provide for them, as all the neighbors talk about how bad a mother she is because she leaves them home alone. You can't think that someone is not loving, just based or judged upon their current state. Nobody knows anybody until you have walked in their shoes.

As I mentioned earlier, what about those who kill and commit terrible crimes upon other's lives, people who lie, cheat, or steal. The Edge of love is a very distant place for them. It is always there for them to turn back to, but for many of them, they've gone so far to the other side that they can no longer see it. Like the saying goes, they're in the woods, but cannot see the forest. They're angrily running through the woods in desperation, wreaking havoc on everything in their paths; the forest is getting thicker, vines are lashing their faces, and they're dehydrated, dark, alone, and lost. They keep running deeper and deeper in desperation because they're trapped; it has become their norm, without realizing that they are simply going deeper and deeper into the forest with no end in sight. Most of these people have been hurt deeply in the past, shunned or mistreated or misunderstood by society. They've been dragged from the Edge of love.. Into the woods they go unwillingly, with nothing but their clothes on, and left to fend for themselves. They are bitter with the world, as they don't understand why they were treated as they were. Why they were made fun of at school, why they were told they would never amount to anything, or why the person they loved hurt them.

We have all at some point in our lives been walking away from the edge into the woods, alone and confused. There will be times where you feel like you are walking into the dark forest or that something is dragging you there. We must always remember that we were carved out of love and we came into a world filled with love. No newborn is born malicious; they're born good, and they're filled with love. The first thing that a baby needs when he is born is human affection. This is why studies have shown that one of the most crucial moments of a newborn's life is in being held by his mother as soon as he takes his first couple of breaths. They need to feel their mother's skin, their mother's warmth, their mother's love. We are born this way! We are born seeking love! And when our mother holds us in her bare chest, we give her love, a love so strong that makes most mothers cry. It's the initiation, the first welcome by the universe of love.

We are born at the Edge of love. At the moment we are born, we are pure, untainted by the evil and indifference that is around us. It's an instinct or a divine gift from the creator, whatever makes sense to you in your belief, but the core of all this is that we are all loving creatures. We are all kind, generous, and caring, all loving, but as we go through life, there are moments where the fog rolls in and we start to walk away from the Edge of love. For certain moments in our lives, we are blind, we cannot see the edge anymore, and we start to walk away from it until we no longer see it or find it. There are moments in our lives when we have walked so far away from it that we simply forget it, and if we keep going on that path, we find ourselves in the dark forest, cold and alone.

We must never forget this Edge: this is where we were born. This is where you were welcomed into the world, and this is where you took your first breaths. I've thought about this edge many times in my life, and I've realized that we can never go back to this specific place. This is a sacred place that we were welcomed to into the universe. A once in a lifetime place that we see once and never get to see again, but this place serves as our beacon; this place becomes our purpose in life. To spend our life feeling and searching the edges of love, so that one day as we lay in our deathbed, we have remained steadfast enough in our quest for this edge, so that we can find this sacred place again as the universe send us off.

Are We There Yet?

As it is our purpose to eventually make it back to that sacred place, it is the journey that is one of the most rewarding. Yes, the goal is to make it there, but the journey is our lives. The part where you can impact the world around you, you can serve the universe's purpose and perform your duty to translate the beauty of the universe through the Rosetta Stone called love. You must use everything the universe has equipped you with, your senses and your mind, to translate the beauty of the universe through love.

It is our civil duty as citizens of the universe to help others see the magic that is around us. We must take them to see the breathtaking view from the top of a mountain, take them swimming on the warm ocean and take them away from the city lights to see the Milky Way galaxy. If you fully experience the world and live in the now, the world is a magical place. Every moment is magical as long as you seek the love in each moment. I understand though, that to feel loving in every second of our lives is impossible, but this is what we should strive for every day. Some of us can live closer to the moment, and for some of us, we only experience slight feelings of being in it. Seeking love in the smallest of places brings about deeper meaning and happiness. Of course this is easy to say, but difficult to do. Remember though, when you appreciate each moment as it is and try to find the love in it consistently, you are walking towards the Edge of love.

This is why we must constantly analyze the moments that shape our thinking. How we judge others, how we interpret the meaning of the world around us. We must keep ourselves in check in going in the right direction, but most importantly of all, enjoy the journey itself.

Signs Along The Road

Countless times in my life, I've wondered what I could do to get closer to love when there were times I was walking away from the Edge. There will be specific signs during those times where you get a wake-up, a call or a sign, and you can either embrace it, learn from it and turn back around, or ignore it. These states will present themselves as a sign that you are being pulled away from the Edge.

Being stuck on the past is one of them. The past is not going to come back; those exact moments are gone, and what's here is now. There have been times in my life when I wasn't content with relationships. I kept comparing them to my past ones, as if somehow that same exact relationship would unfold again. It ruined many of my relationships because I was so stuck on wanting it to be the same. That was never going to happen; I was a different age, a completely different person, in a completely different stage of life, and yet somehow, it still affected my life. This was a sign for me that I was walking away from the Edge of love.

I was withholding giving my love freely to others because I couldn't see love. My version of love was very different because I was looking for that specific type of love. It became hard for me to see beauty until I realized this. I was not seeing the rest of the beauty that, consistently, the universe tried to show me. Things would have to be very out of the ordinary for me to experience love. I was translating love as if only knowing a couple letters of the Rosetta Stone. I was translating love based on one kind of love, and I could not understand all others.

This is why, when a loved one passes away, people undergo so much pain, and on many occasions, change the way they perceive their world as a result. A kind of love that they have known for a long time is gone forever – many become depressed or angry towards the world. They are lost, they can no longer see love around them because they're looking for that person's love that is no longer there. We are creatures of habit, and it's hard for us to adapt to change. This is why, when we move away from our friends and family to a new place, it can be hard to adjust; it can be hard to find the love of that new place.

See how one event can change someone's interpretation of the world. This happens to many of us, as we base our lives on specific past events that hold us hostage, and illiterate to the love around us. We take the love that we learned in the past and use that to translate the love that we receive in our present day. Someone can be showing us a loving gesture and we either don't see it as a loving one or it doesn't touch our heart. Why? Because it's like trying to understand someone speaking Italian when you only know English; you're not understanding their language, not comprehending their love. This happens often because we are stuck in the past – we're stuck in a state of being where it's not going to come back. You must release that thinking and use that love that you learned, and teach it to others as you also learn the rest of the letters of the Rosetta Stone of love.

When you let go and decide to move forward, you have now opened yourself up for beauty and love to enter you again. It becomes easier to see that the simple things are the ones that actually fill you heart with the most love. You no longer need to depend on tangible things to fill your heart with love; you can relax, you don't have to go on rampages seeking where the love is. The world around you starts to make you content, as you have been transformed, and you start walking towards the Edge of love again.

Take some time and sit alone by yourself: go outside, sit in the grass, and think about some of the past you might be holding onto that is shaping your current life. Learn the loves, embrace them, and never forget them – they will always be part of your life – but open up yourself to the beauty and love around you again. Free up your heart and experience the love from your friends, parents, strangers, and the natural world, thinking about the role nature plays in our world and how it constantly gives to us in our lives.

Inside You

Many of us like to fall victim to the world around us and believe that the reason we are not feeling love is because others don't love us. In this case, we believe that love comes from the outside and not the inside. As stated earlier, you were born full of love and it is up to you to feel the love, so you shouldn't blame others for the lack of love you experience because your love should not be decided by somebody else, it should be decided by you. This is why someone's parents can love them unconditionally, and yet they can't seem to feel it. How come you can love someone you've never even met personally? Because love comes from within you, as you decide how to translate the love around you. Nobody can force their love on you if you don't let it in; you have to be open and have room for it.

Seeing the concept of love in this manner is very empowering. It frees you from the belief that you have to depend on any one particular person or object to fill your heart with love. You are free to choose how you want love to enter your soul and how you want to give it. That is the freedom we all have. This is the way the universe was designed. If we depended on others to fill our share of love, we would all be prisoners of each other and love would not truly exist. You have to remember that you're in control of the door – you're in control of how much love comes into your life.

When we open ourselves up to other forms of love, such as the beauty of nature, the simple nice gesture from a stranger, or to the love of a compassionate act and gratitude, our heart tends to fill with love much faster and with less effort. Our measure of love does not have to depend on one particular person or certain events in our lives. We become stronger, we adjust to change more rapidly, and we become more accepting. The world essentially lights up and our perception changes. We can also walk more in the moment, as love keeps us awake, passionate and alive. No longer do we have to depend on the past for love and comfort.

Love Has to Flow

Remember, I said earlier that the universe uses us as an instrument to translate the beauty and the world that is around us. We constantly project the beauty that we see through our senses. If you genuinely feel love, your body language lets others know you are happy, your actions let others feel your love inside, your words let others know that love exists, and your energy will let others know that love is in the air. We are all projections of our love, we must let love flow in and we must also let it flow out.

For example, if someone we love breaks up with us, we're hurt, we become broken, and we become a dam for love. It is normal for us to store this love that used to flow in and out of our soul. We are in a critical point of life, that love is no longer flowing in, so we hold onto it for as long as we can. We essentially become closed and like water that sits around without flow, that love inside becomes stagnant and no longer useful. Love doesn't come in and love doesn't come out. We are just holding on for dear life. It becomes impossible for anyone to love us and for us to love them. One needs to be willing to let go of that love; you're going to feel sad and scared, but this is just a sign that you're opening up yourself again and letting love flow through you.

We must be mindfully aware when we become closed. This usually happens after a traumatic event occurs in our life. We have to accept that this is a normal stage of life. We will become closed, and it is in our natural instincts for our minds to do this, as our minds are always trying to protect us from sadness. In doing this, the mind hampers our ability to let love out, and this becomes our defense mechanism. Once you are aware that this is happening, you have to force yourself to open up to the existing world around you and remain open, and love will take care of the rest. Love will start flowing in many forms. You might not know where you will be receiving it from, but as long as you are letting love flow out freely, it will come in, and in many different ways.

Love and Gratitude

Gratitude is one of the most powerful actions one can engage to let love flow in. It becomes very difficult to have a sense of gratitude when we don't set time aside during our day to think about the things we are thankful to have in our lives.

Thoughts are always racing in our heads… What am I going to cook today? I need to call the warehouse and see how our numbers look. Why did that person look at me like that? Millions of thoughts flood our minds during the day, so much so that many of us never really sit and realize how blessed we are. We don't focus on the so-called haves; we focus on what we need. Our brains are constantly analyzing the past and the future because – if we think in the simplest terms, about what our minds primary job once our physical (safety, food, shelter) needs are met.. Our happiness becomes the key element for that goal. Instinctually our brains have developed with the goal of protecting us from everything that might possibly cause us harm, and to seek ways to keep us happy. Can you imagine how difficult of a job that would be?

Our brain has to constantly analyze everything around us in the present, think about all the different situations in the past so that we don't do the same things that caused us sadness, and to look for the instances that made us happy. It also has to think and somehow predict future outcomes that will make us happier, and keep us from risky situations, when most of the time, they're just irrational assumptions regarding future events. In all this, there's usually no room to actually stop and think about the greatness that presently exists in us. Many of us only take time during the holidays to say one or two things we are thankful for. And we tend to pray for things to either happen or not happen to us. Instead of saying thanks for all of our blessings and good fortunes.

It becomes necessary to take time out of our busy lives and recognize these gifts that we tend to forget and take for granted. You have to force yourself to do this, because your mind has an impossible task at hand and has no extra time for this objective on a moment-by-moment instinctive basis. We have to sit down and even write out what we are thankful for. We have to make a list of these things and read them constantly to remind us of the love that does exist in our lives, and the love that we have to remain open to.

Make a list of everything you love – memories, people in your life, places you've been to, things you have accomplished, the fact that you have food and water available to you, your home, your car, and most importantly, characteristics about yourself that you cherish. You want to list the things that help you feel the love that is already within your soul. You want this list to serve as a constant reminder to you of the love that you already have. We tend to focus on what we don't have, as we are constantly seeking the new, the next best thing, but we forget all the worthy things that currently happen in our lives. Go over this list regularly and add new things you come up with. Picture each item in your mind and feel the love awaken from your heart.

As you go through your day, remember to always look for things that bring you love… the smile from the cashier, the old couple holding hands, the feeling you get when you see someone you love or when your child hugs you. It's the little things that we must get into a habit of seeing, and most importantly of all, being aware of. We need to be aware when we are not allowing the feeling of love to flow into our hearts. When you feel blocked, go back to your list if you need to; listen to your favorite song, go on a walk by yourself, and just focus on your breathing and try to find beauty in something that catches your eye. We are not perfect, so these blocks will come in from time to time, but if you keep to your gratitude list and constantly choose thoughts, words, and actions that are in alignment with your love, it will become easier to release the block each time.

Blocks

There are many things that block the flow of love within us. These are moments that take us away from love that put us in a state where love is non-existent. These are triggers that automatically close your heart and change your inner love chemistry. One factor that creates blocks is judgments. We are all guilty of making them. As a natural instinctual mechanism, we judge others to protect ourselves. We need to know who someone is and if they are of interest to us. The problem becomes when we move from this to judging people without any factual information. 99% of the time, we are completely wrong. We are actually just making up a story in our head, based on someone's appearance and what little information we've gathered about them. They're too quiet or they're too nice, they dress too preppy or they must be poor. We are, in essence, lying about the person we're judging. Loving and making irrational assumptions about someone just don't go together. This puts us in a state of discomfort and mistrust.

I was on a flight one day, and we were waiting for the cabin's door to close. At the last minute, this man comes barging into the plane with a large carry-on duffle bag and a plastic bag filled with a burger and fries smell. The man sat behind me and I felt that my chair kept getting kicked or moved. Anyway, without me realizing it, my mind was already making up a story about this guy. Always late to everything, out of shape so that he eats fast food all the time, doesn't care about other people, rude and annoying. Wow, I literally did that in the span of thirty seconds. How did I know all this? The chair antics kept happening and I did a quick look back with an unhappy expression on my face. My feelings since that man had walked in had changed. I felt bothered, frustrated, and was definitely not feeling any love at that moment – I was blocked. Okay, well, it ended, we took off, and I kept reading my book. When the flight attendant passed by to offer snacks and drinks, I heard him asking for two beers. Again, my mind started, "this guy is a drunk who orders two beers for himself at the same time on a plane?" I thought.

All of a sudden, I felt a tap on my shoulder, and it's the guy. "Oh man, what does he want now?" I turned around and he handed me a beer with a sticky note on it where he had written: "sorry for the crazy chair antics, I was trying to stuff my bag under the chair, but couldn't get it in there, take this beer as my apology". Wow, foot in mouth... Was I embarrassed? I felt so bad that I'd made those assumptions about a man I hadn't even talked to. I'd been wrong about everything. I talked to him afterwards and he told me he was flying in for a mountain bike training event, and he ended up being an awesome interesting guy. I think it was the first time I realized how quick and wrong I really was in judging others.

We must refrain from judging other people. It automatically blocks the flow of love through us. If you are going to judge someone, judge them in a positive way. "Man, this poor guy must have had a short connection and had just enough time to get some fast food – how can I help him out?" Why didn't I just think about it in this way from the beginning? It would have been far more helpful for both him and I. Judging someone in a negative way does absolutely nothing for you. It puts you in a negative state and the help or encouragement that the other person might need actually never comes because of a wrong judgment.

Now, if we are so harsh and quick to judge others, imagine how hard we judge ourselves. We are constantly analyzing our appearances and actions. Often times though, we say some pretty harsh things which we would never even tell a stranger. There have been times of frustration for me where I hated myself, hated myself for mistakes I made in the past, for not talking enough, for being introverted at times, for not taking enough risks, for taking too many risks, for having too much fun, and for not having enough fun. It's crazy, the stuff our minds tell us about ourselves. It's unbelievable that all of us, at one point or another, have looked in the mirror and said to ourselves that we didn't like something about our appearances, or that we weren't good-looking enough. Or that we were never going to achieve our dreams.

Our minds can be our greatest enemies at times. It can be our greatest liar or our greatest motivator. It's constantly narrating a story about our lives and never forgets to tell us what's wrong about ourselves in the process. How can we let love flow through us if we can't even love ourselves? We must be aware of this. Aware of the thoughts we say about ourselves; instead of focusing on our bad qualities, we need to be our biggest cheerleader. We must constantly speak great things to ourselves. This is why we must listen and read motivational material, because society is always good about telling us what's wrong with ourselves. If you don't even talk positively to yourself, imagine the impact the world around you has. Anytime you're feeling weak or talk badly about yourself, think about the good qualities that you have. What have you done for others? You are not what your negative mind says you are. We are all human beings with faults, dreams, and the desire to be loved and give love.

Uncertainty Loves Control

One of the biggest enemies of love is uncertainty. No one can predict the future, but regardless, we all try to control it as much as we believe we can. The need to control the future is one of the biggest contributors to driving people away from the Edge of love. Trying to control the future is like trying to predict every traffic light on your way to work. It's going to be a lot of work, and it's going to disappoint you when you hit a red light, and you are going to become very frustrated with yourself and the world around you.

Throughout our lives, we tend to try and control situations to go the way we want them to go. For example, we might wear a certain type of clothing to hopefully make the other person think in a certain way about us; we might talk in a certain way to convince the other person to act the way we want them to, and sometimes we lie to others or ourselves to make something look how we want it to appear. We make posts on social media to make others think about our life in a way that we want to be portrayed. We sometimes pursue a career we don't even like, but which has a higher certainty for a bigger paycheck or higher status.

Uncertainty is one of the main drivers of people's lives today. It becomes a constant battle, a constant game, and some of us realize on our deathbeds that our whole lives have been driven just based on the fear of uncertainty. When we try to control everything around us, life starts to become more materialistic, and in a way loses its color. The pursuit of control over uncertainty keeps us from the present, keeps us blind to the love around us, and keeps us walking away from the Edge of love.

When we try to control others and they don't behave how we want them to, we might develop anger. We lose the potential for love from others as we might be too blind to see their beauty, because we are in a constant quest to make people behave a certain way, and if they don't, we often simply write them off. This is one reason why racism exists, this is why hate and anger towards others exists. We are all different, we all grew up in different scenes of life, in different cultures, in different neighborhoods, with different parents, with different religions, with different personalities and different Edges of love. How can we expect others to act as we think they will act? It's impossible! Trying to control others robs us of being in the present, along with the potential to see the existing opportunities and love around us.

So much weight is lifted off our shoulders when we let go of the need to control others' actions. This liberates us from being let down or proven wrong. It gives us a different aspect of people and situations. It opens us to the harmony of the universe. The universe revolves around uncertainty. Every snowflake that falls is a different shape, every cloud that forms is unique, and no two fingerprints are ever alike. The world speaks to us in so many simple concepts that we just don't seem to understand. We have lost the sense that we are part of the world and the interconnection we have with each other. We have lost the ability to see the symbols that the universe shows us every day.

We have lost the ability to accept that uncertainty is part of our lives because it has been our purpose to try and control all aspects of the natural world. We have been so good at predicting and controlling other natural aspects of daily life, such as weather prediction; we have been able to control food production so that we can eat tomatoes year-round, marketers predict what we want to buy, rivers have been dammed, corporate institutions have been compartmentalized with cubicles and climbing the corporate ladder mentality.. We are used to control, as it makes us feel safe. Change and uncertainty bring a sinking feeling in our stomachs, a tightness in our chests. Uncertainty is the reason why you lose trust in others, in yourself, and in love. Your life starts walking in a thin line of uncertainty, where it's very easy to fall. What if you didn't have to walk on this thin line all the time? How would you feel? Would you be more open to change? More open to love?

In life, the only thing that you can work to control is your own actions and your perception of others. History has proven, time and time again, that people inherently cannot be controlled. Your life was not meant to be controlled by others. Whatever your belief is, the universe, the Supreme Being, or God did not make us to be controlled by any particular thing. You are meant to live in harmony with all creatures around you, which is the only way to ensure our survival and our individual love. Governments in the past have tried to control people by suppressing them, but no matter how hard they've tried, people tend to fight back for that harmony. It's in your blood, as it's in the natural order of the world for things to coexist in harmony. Anywhere in the world where people are being suppressed or controlled, there's always a fire burning in someone's heart to fight back.

You must let go of that need to control; you must open up your heart and believe in yourself and others. Most important of all, you must go through life with the belief in love. You must use love as your shield, when walking in the shadow of fear and in the uncertainty of the new. Don't use your life to focus on people and situations behaving in a certain way; rather, focus on how you can apply your love to the world around you.

Part Three- Fear: The Gatekeeper of Dreams

"Everything you want is on the other side of fear."
-Jack Canfield

As I've gotten older – life has taught me a lesson time and time again, and yet I often forget it. Fear is the destroyer of dreams. Fear has caused millions of people to die with their hopes and dreams still in their minds. It's crazy to think that fear is an actual feeling which we feel, but many times, it feels like someone is actually speaking to us. You could have the greatest idea in the world, but fear could stop you in your tracks and make you feel that you have the worst idea in the world. Why do we have this feeling that impacts us in such a negative way? Why does fear even exist? Why do we let a feeling dictate our dreams and our lives? After all, it is just a feeling, right?

All humans experience fear, and whether you call it instinctual or self-evoked, fear is fear. Fear is the feeling that makes you feel that something or someone is threatening to you, something which has the potential to cause you physical harm or discomfort. Fear started out as a protective mechanism to keep us safe from potential danger. Just like other animals are fearful when they see a predator or keep a constant watch for every noise or smell they detect that might signal a potential threat. It was also instinctually instilled in us to keep us safe from other predators. Yes, thousands of years ago, early humans were prey to other large carnivores. The instinct of fear ensured our survival. It made humans more careful, more aware of their surroundings; fear, in a sense, brought us together. Fear pushed humans to be creative and develop ways to stay safe. It's one of the factors involved in why people gathered in places and created small tribes – to lessen the fear of trying to survive in the world alone.

Fear, for thousands of years, kept us safe, but we are at a time where fear is no longer used for the same purposes on a regular basis.

We now are in fear of being fired from our jobs, not getting into the colleges we want, not saying the right thing at company meetings, or not being liked by others. Fear is no longer there to protect us from a predator; for many people, physical survival is not an issue anymore, as we don't have any actual sabretooth tigers hiding in caves and waiting for a meal, but it still functions to keep us away from discomfort or pain. The things that cause us danger are different now. Fear mostly serves to protect us emotionally. It keeps you from going into a place that might cause you some emotional hurt or, sometimes, physical pain. It's just trying to ensure your survival. Fear, in this case, is your friend and your protector.

The problem becomes when it starts protecting us from all aspects of our lives. It literally takes over our life choices. Anytime there is an unknown, fear automatically tries to decide for you, "No! You don't know what's going to happen". Fear has always tried to predict the future by looking for all the bad things that could possibly happen to us. It's constantly scanning for people and situations that might cause us potential harm. It's looking for the worst case scenario, anticipating every bad thing that could happen to us along the way. It's really just looking out for us in an extreme way.

What happens when a child grows up in a constantly controlling or fearful environment, where he's told by his parents... don't touch that, don't do this, don't say this, don't go over there, don't learn this, come here, go there, study this, wear this, don't wear that. Everything he does has a potential for an apprehensive 'no' from his parents. His parents are not necessarily bad people – they might just be over-protective due to some past experiences they have had or the way they were raised, but their child starts to question himself and assume that whatever he's going to do might be harmful to him. He becomes scared of the world around him. He becomes frozen by fear. It's difficult for him to express himself – he becomes scared to laugh, scared to speak his mind, or scared to stand up for what he believes. Therefore, his parents, and later society, have instilled in him such a strong concept of fear and caution that the child grows up and, even as an adult, still somehow has the same fears that have affected his whole life.

This is how fear has developed in our senses. It started out as basic instinct to protect us from real imminent danger, transitioning into scaring us from doing the very things we love or might really enjoy (if we tried them). Fear has been magnified by our surroundings. It's easier to conform than to go outside the lines and go on your own path. It's easier and less scary to hike to a place for which the path has already been paved, where there's a bathroom, a concession stand, and fences to keep you from going outside of the designated viewing area. The drawback in going this route is that you don't really get to experience all the feelings of a real hiking adventure, and to a place where few people have been. The path is not marked, and sometimes you feel alone so you have to face many fears, but you have to face them and keep going. There are many unknowns, but you get to really live the hike. You get to see beauty, you feel a sense of purpose during the journey, you feel excitement, you feel appreciative, you live more in the moment, and you get to learn more about yourself and others. Now, which path seems more fulfilling?

Fear, Our Beacon

As I stated earlier, we must look for love and opportunity in all aspects of our lives as this tends to get us closer to the Edge of love. In order to live more fulfilled lives, we must not look at fear as our enemy or as a physical emotion that draws us farther from our humanity, instead we need to look at fear as a beacon in our lives. Fear, most of the time is going to keep us from doing something new, things that require work and mental input. Fear wants us to conserve our energy, keep our feelings from fluctuating invariably, and keep you from change and the unknown. To fear, the new and the unknown are two very scary places. It doesn't know how much energy you are going to have to spend, how emotionally changed you will be. It wants to keep life stable for you. It's like being an animal inside a fence. You get fed, nothing out of the ordinary happens, you don't have to worry about predators, and you live a relatively stable life. The thing you give up, though, for that comfort and assurance, is seeing the rest of the world outside of the fence. You miss out on all the experiences that come with interacting with an ever-changing world, full of all kinds of beauty and emotions that come with living on the Edge of fear.

We must step outside of the fence to begin to experience life outside of the shadow of fear and realize that the things which scare us tend to be the ones that we should be doing, as long as they are constructive, positive, and speak to our heart. We must do the things that give our stomach butterflies when you picture that dream in your mind. Everything new and unknown tends to gives us the feeling of fear. Remember that girl or guy you liked? What did you feel when you thought about them? Happy, excited, butterflies? What did you feel when you thought about talking to them? Anxiety, denial, fear? This is how fear operates. So, what must you do? Should you just forget about them? You can't. Should you just go on, the rest of your life, not asking them out because you might get your feelings hurt? You might think you're not good enough? You might think he/she might not like your type?

This is what happens daily in just this specific part of life. Imagine all the other aspects of our daily lives. The same thing happens to us when we think about taking a different journey, going to an unknown place, making art that we are passionate about, and following our dreams. Fear will always be there as a beacon, letting you know that it's worth doing. I love the quote by Eddie Rickenbacker— "Courage is about doing what you're afraid to do. There can be no courage unless you're scared." The courage to stand up to our fears, strengthens the more we do the things that scare us.

If the things you want to do don't raise a feeling of various emotions inside, then they're not going to be able to sustain your journey mentally. We must feel fear in order to know where to walk to. The actions that you feel fear or resistance towards are the ones that you should focus on – again, as long as they are positive, constructive, and speak to your heart with love. We must always remember to analyze the fear you feel inside, and not just be quick to react to it. Accept it, study it, and ask ourselves the questions as to why we are feeling that fear. Write those answers down and see if the feeling of fear makes sense or is logical. Most of the time, fear paints an illogical story line that has not even happened. Think about that fearful story that plays out in your head. Is it logical? Is it realistic? Or does it conflict with your heart? We must welcome fear as part of our guidance system in life. Look beyond the fear and see what you can accomplish by going past it. When you think about the positive outcomes that come from moving past the fear, and continuing to follow your heart despite the feelings of fear you experience, it will be easier to continue your journey into the new and the unknown. Fear is just part of the human experience. Walk close to the Edge of fear at all times; make it your friend, your guide, and your beacon to what is worth pursuing in your heart.

Is it your intention to become fit again, to begin a healthy lifestyle? When people start on this journey to change their lives, fear starts to set in. Your fears start to talk and develop a story. You're not fit enough to go to the gym, and when are you going to find the time? You're going to have to give up on all the good things you like to eat, you're going to miss time with your family and friends, and isn't that selfish of you, to focus on your appearance? You're not going to have enough energy to do all of this, and on and on. See what fear is doing? It wants to keep you stable, at bay, away from change, away from the unknown. This still happens to me before I go to the gym, as sometimes I'll look for an excuse to get out of going. It was very hard in the beginning, but after a while, I learned and expected those thoughts in my mind. The more I pushed past those fearful thoughts and excuses my mind made up, the easier it was for me to walk past fear. I began to embrace fear as letting me know what I should be doing. Anytime I found myself making up excuses or thoughts on why I shouldn't go to the gym or for a run, it always reminded me to do the opposite and face the fear. This applies to all aspects of our lives; the more we push past fear and use it as our guide, the more natural it becomes to move past it.

The Voice in The Dark Forest

Jad Abumrad is the radio host and producer for *Radio Lab*. I love this guy, as he has reinvented the way stories on the radio are told. It's hard for our generation to listen to stories on the radio because we are inundated with so many other media sources, such as the internet and television. Jad has made his show attractive to our generation, by reinventing the way stories are told. When I first listened to him, I always saw him as this great innovator with the perfect radio voice. When we admire someone famous or an accomplished person, we often see them as ones with a unique skill. Rarely do we ever think about the struggles that they went through to get there. It's hard to relate and understand them, because seldom do people's stories come up, as we often just see the final product or the glitter and the gold, yet their stories of struggle and courage to reach a certain dream is often overlooked or unheard.

I went to see Jad, for the first time, when he was talking to a group of college students. As he came out on stage, I thought, "man, there's the real guy" – still in awe of seeing someone I listened to on the radio, but had never even known what he looked like. All I knew was his voice and his radio show.

He started to talk about his early career and all the struggles he had in radio for many years. He simplified his story by talking about the feelings of fear he encountered along the way. He said he'd never thought he had a radio voice. He always compared himself to other hosts and thought that his voice would never be good for radio. Jad still pursued his dream of having his own radio show despite all the fears he felt. He explained the beginning of his career as being in a dark forest, alone. Every new unknown was an indescribably crazy feeling in his stomach; every footstep he took in the dark forest brought new fears. The first time he spoke on radio, he felt so much anxiety that he could barely talk, but after a couple of minutes, that fearful feeling started to go away. He explained that every time he encountered something new, he found himself in the dark forest, walking in fear and alone, but after a while, the forest stopped being so dark and scary, and would only remain there for a few minutes. Each time he faced his fears, the time he spent in the dark forest seemed less and less, and he became used to it. Jad stated that, every day he gets these feelings, but he embraces them as a sign that he's moving towards courage and his dreams.

Remember your first day in a new school? The fear of meeting new people, the fear of being the new kid in school, and the fear of what people would judge you to be. You still pushed on and, after a couple of days passed, it didn't seem so bad. You started to meet new friends, you were no longer the new kid in school, and those fears started to disappear. This is the same concept as Jad's story. The new school represented the dark forest, and you felt alone and scared, but after a while, the forest stopped being as scary, and your eyes adjusted to the darkness and it stopped being as dark. You must always remember that this is part of change: fear will always be there, but you must see it as a challenge to get past this wall of fear and see what's on the other side.

Pay a Visit to Fear

Fear tends to live in the places where your ideas and your self-purpose reside. It makes that area look dark and scary, as it doesn't want you to go there. It makes it look very far away sometimes, makes it seem like the journey there is impossible, and it's so powerful that it even uses the fear of others to keep you from going. Once you realize this, though, you quickly become more powerful than fear itself. You see fear for what it is; you accept it, and you say, "hey, I know you are there", and it can do whatever tricks it wants, but it cannot stop you physically. It can do no physical action to actually keep you from moving past it and continuing on your path. See how powerful you become.

The problem is that many of us don't accept fear: we don't like the feeling of it, so as soon as it pops up, we turn right back around. When you see it, acknowledge that it's always going to be there, saying the same imaginative story. The more you get to know it and accept it, the more it becomes your ally. We must see it through and look at fear in the utmost realistic way. It's just an instinctual emotion that has been put on overdrive.

Take the time to feel the fear; get to know your own and pay a visit to those places where it resides. Go to those places and keep walking towards the light in the far distance of your mind, and don't pay any mind to the darkness around you, as you will soon get to the light. Once you pay a visit to one, keep visiting the others. See the fear in each one of those places and just continue to move forward. As you do this, fear around your ideas and purpose will start to be less noticeable. It will always be there, but eventually, it doesn't say as much to you anymore. It starts to give up, it becomes lazier and less important. It rarely tries to put fear in you anymore, and it waits till you become weak to strike again. It constantly looks for those weak moments in your life, and then decides to strike with all its might, but this time you will be ready for it, and you become stronger… the more you beat fear, itself.

It took me a long time to come to this realization in myself. As to how much fear was driving my life. I was constantly afraid to follow my ideas and the purpose I believed I had. I couldn't bear the feeling of fear. It always somehow talked me out of walking on the path where I could see the light. When I reflect on my teen years, I regularly followed my heart. If there was something I wanted to do, I did it. I took risks and walked along the Edge of fear. As I got older, fear started to take a hold of me. I became comfortable, afraid of change, afraid of failure, and afraid of following the light in my heart. As time went by, I saw how different I became as a person because of fear. I started to remember who I was when I was young. I had had no cares in the world, and I'd let myself live on all edges of my life. I hadn't restrained my ideas and feelings. I'd followed my heart. When I realized fear had taken a hold of me, I asked myself why I had changed. I then understood that fear had started taking the wheel for my life.

When we're young, we tend to be very free; we have a tendency to walk on the Edge of love and fear because many of us haven't been hurt deeply by the world around us. As we start to enter our adult lives, we are hurt. Hurt by love, hurt by our dreams, hurt by our purposes, and hurt by our ideas. The very first few hits, we are shocked. Why did that happen to me, you ask? You're brought to an uncomfortable place and your mind jots it down. As time goes by, we feel disappointment and are let down by ourselves and others. We start to become fearful of the world around us and we start shutting down. We no longer step outside of our comfort zone. We lay down our swords and begin living our life in a small way to avoid any deviations in our emotions.

This is how fear took a hold of me, but I'm grateful for that experience. If I never would have experienced that on an extreme level, where I could barely get out of bed to face the world or sit at my desk – clicking my pen over and over with no sense of purpose – or experience my older brother's death, I might have not realized how fear was impacting my life. Once I saw fear for what it was, and the purpose it had in my life, I understood it better – I got to know it and saw the fraud that it was. We are all duped by fear – it's the greatest con artist in the world – but once you see its true self, it loses its power.

I believe that the greatest inventors and people that have moved our world forward, are those who said yes when the rest of the world told them no, people who fought for injustice when no one else would fight, these people were able to understand fear, but consistently facing it. They knew its presence, but kept walking in the path of darkness, with their eyes fixed straight to the light shining at the end of the path. It becomes easier to follow the things in which your heart calls on you for, once you fully understand that. See the capabilities? You just have to keep walking and trust your heart, as it will always get you through to the other side.

Since we know that fear often times will be casting a shadow on our thoughts and ideas, we have to be prepared to keep walking down the darkened path, regardless of what fear is saying to you. The light that you see at the far end of the path is what you focus on.

Faith Kills Fear

One of the greatest weapons we can use against fear is our faith. Nobody ever accomplished a great feat without believing in themselves. When you decide to face your fears in order to get to your dreams, you will be traveling on a dark path with fear by your side, telling you to turn back, and if it's something you truly desire, there will be times when you are traveling on that path and then it suddenly becomes very dark. Where the light at the far end of the path by which your dream resides is no longer visible... it's helpful to bring a flashlight. That flashlight is your faith. When the light from your dreams starts to get dim and you are contemplating turning back, you have to pull out your faith so it can help shine a little bit of light on the path so you can keep going. Sometimes, your faith is the only thing that you can rely on in order for you to keep walking on the darkened path.

There were times in my life where certain things were calling my heart, yet I chose not to pursue them further because of fear. I strongly believed in them, yet I stopped and turned back when the path got dark and difficult. As I took action on my dreams, on the things that kept me walking along the Edge of love, it wasn't until I developed faith in them and myself that I started to get past the darkness and get closer to the light. There's going to be those moments where, even if you have started facing your fears, in order to live the life that you know is right in your heart, fear will sometimes get to you along the way and cause you to turn back. This is where our faith comes in. At times you will have to walk blindly with the world against you, and you will ask yourself why you are doing it, and you must go to your faith. Your faith is the belief in yourself and the universe. Have the belief that, if you take action and follow your heart, those dreams will be attained as long as you remain steadfast through your journey there. When you hit a block in the road, keep going, and if the world tells you otherwise and you have faith in your dream, keep pushing.

When I started writing this book, I told myself that I would write every day, no matter what. Tired, things to do or with no motivation, I said I would still sit down and think about ideas and topics or write, even if it was just a couple sentences. I knew that writing a book was not going to be an easy journey. I knew fear was going to try and throw at me whatever it took to get me to stop.

I had to figure out a way to get past this. I assumed that if I told myself I had to write every day, no matter what, before I even started to write, it was going to get rid of how those excuses would get to me and potentially end with me not writing the book. There have been times when it's 11pm at night and I'm tired from work. And I have said to myself, "I'll just write more tomorrow and make up for not writing today", or, "tomorrow I will be able to better put my thoughts on paper", but I quickly realize this excuse based thinking was happening, and I would say to myself "you're about to break your promise to yourself". I would get up. This promise has been based on faith. I know that if I keep writing every day, eventually I will finish the book and it would enable me to get my thoughts out to the world. If I had to start believing in anything, I had to start with myself. I had to keep my promise to myself that I would write every day. And so, every day I write, whether I come home exhausted from work or sitting at an airport waiting for a flight: I write. It has started to become part of my everyday life. After some time, writing has become easier, and I feel more joy in my life; things I observe during the day inspire me because I feel that deep down I'm following my heart. You have to give yourself a fail-safe, something that you can use in your journey that is guaranteed to keep you going forward.

As I stated in the previous chapter: the majority of the things we do in life, we tend to do it for love. Many times, we're doing something for our spouse, our children, our friends, and even the world. At times, there's a bigger reason than the actual reason we believe we have as a purpose. Before you start your journey, be clear on why you are going along that path. Create a rock, something that is indestructible compared to fear, and that you can always resort to during the dark times. You simply cannot just rely on your will power, because many times, fear is stronger than will power. You must eliminate that part of the equation so that you move forward with more resistance to turning back.

Take, for example, religion. Many religions are based on faith. In order to have faith, you need belief and love in a certain entity or what it stands for. Often times, the reason we follow a certain religion or cause, is because something about it resonates with our heart or how we interpret the world around us.. Whether that being to us is God, Jesus, Allah, Buddha, or universal nature, one becomes our rock. This is the very essence of how we walk along faith and how life shows us how to walk along fear. We cannot have faith without belief or action; therefore, in times where your faith might be questioned, you can resort to something that embodies what your heart believes. Our brains have to react quickly to fear and revert back to something that automatically lets us know why we chose to go on our personal journeys.

This is true for all those who face fear on their journeys. For the father who is working long hours in his make-shift studio basement to get his invention off the ground, to give his family a better standard of living. For the mother who is working extra shifts at her job to help her daughter pay for college. For Dr. Martin Luther King, Jr. who endured severe opposition, ridicule, and death threats as he fought for what he believed was right in his heart and the dream that one day his children would grow up in a nation where they wouldn't be judged by the color of their skin, but by the content of their character.

If you ever want to see the embodiment of faith, watch Dr. Martin Luther King, Jr.'s speech, "I Have a Dream". He showed up at one of the largest demonstrations ever recorded at our nation's capital to speak. A situation like this could bring fear to even the strongest of champions. The fear must have been immense. When you watch the beginning of his "I Have a Dream" speech, you can hear his voice tremble a bit; his face expression shows fear, and perhaps the feeling of being overwhelmed, but he reverts back to his rock, his dream… and then faces fear straight on and voices a speech that moved a whole nation. He moved past the fear because of how strong his faith was in that his dream would come true… he just had to get past the fear. Dr. King becomes a legendary person once you see that speech, but he was equipped with the same physical attributes as everyone else. The one thing Dr. King did differently is that he faced great fear, where most would succumb to it and give up on the journey. I like to mention Dr. King because he is a perfect example of someone who walked along the Edge of fear. He constantly felt for the edges, as those would get him closer to his dream.

We all have this power available to us. We have the power to do great things, but we must not be afraid of fear; we must be willing to accept it, understand it, and then decide to move forward. In any endeavor your heart gravitates towards, you will likely feel some sort of fear. This is the natural process, as change is scary, breaking habits is hard, and thinking outside of the box can be frightening, and sometimes you question your very own being, but you must move forward as long as you are following your heart, like Dr. King did.

Finding Purpose By Walking Alongside Fear

When we are young, often times we don't truly think much about what we want to do in life as a job or our dreams. Children often get asked what they want to be, but in general our thinking has not developed enough to truly know what it is. We are too busy exploring and feeling the world around us. I was always pushing the limits of change, adventure, risk, athleticism, and love. I was passionate about my life and everything that was happening around me. Even the bad experiences... I embraced them and experienced them, and then I moved on and continued experiencing life. Life didn't seem like work. Everything just flowed naturally, but I was excited for what new experience the next day would bring. As I grew older, though, I started to think about my purpose in life; what was I meant to do? What gift was I supposed to give to the world?

We all have these critical moments in our lives. Where we think about what our purposes should be. Even if just for a moment, we dream. We are dreamers by nature. We dream in our sleep. There are those moments where your purpose calls on you. All those experiences that you had when you were young, up until now, have added up to your purpose. Everything you have learned, everything you've felt, touched, listened, spoken to, fought, loved, and cherished, has built your purpose – one by one. When that purpose tries to speak to our hearts, we either follow it or turn our backs to it. Sometimes, our purpose changes later in life, but many of us choose not to follow it. In many instances, as we grow up, the world instills fear in us, so much that it has become hard to even trust our own heart.

When we were young, we tended to trust our hearts. We did wild and crazy things for love. Sometimes even sneaking out of our parents' house to just meet your girlfriend/boyfriend at a park. Showed up early to practice and played with passion during our games. Many of the things we did, we did it with passion. Trying to make the squad so we could play the sport we loved or the instrument that made our heart sing. To graduate high school/college, to make our parents proud, to find our purpose in the world and to find someone to love. We didn't know that fear would play such an integral part in pushing us away from following our purposes and following our hearts. Once we entered adulthood, life sort of changed us a bit. Society hardened us to the point where it became hard to listen to our hearts. We stopped walking along the Edge of love. We let life move us from the Edge of fear. We became scared to face the edge. The thought of walking up to that edge and facing it became terrifying. When we let fear drag us from the edges, we lose our love for the world. The world becomes cold, monotonous, and inactive. We settle and become like the animal inside the fence. We are fed and kept from danger, but we lose out on experiencing the world in its entirety.

You stop having a passion and stop following your heart. I've experienced it and have also seen others go through the same process. It becomes an uneasy feeling in our heart. Like, what's my purpose? My life's work can't be just sitting at this desk, doing mind numbing work. It's an indescribable feeling that sneaks up on us at times and reminds us that we are not following our hearts. That feeling can make us look at our lives in a very different way. A meaningless way. The world starts to lose its color. Sometimes we blame ourselves, take out that frustration on the world around us, and lose out on the present moment. Society constantly tells you to follow your heart, to follow your purpose. The problem is, that purpose becomes a physical thing. You have a purpose to buy a nice house, a nice car, make a lot of money, and be important. Purpose becomes this thing that we purchase.

During our young years, our purpose couldn't be bought. We had to study, we had to practice, we had to run, we had to take risks, we had to get hurt, and we had to love. Purpose was something from the heart. We all have different purposes in our lives, but our main purpose that was instilled in us was to love. Whether it is shown by making art, standing up for a cause, or doing it for someone you love. Your purpose is to do the things that speak to your heart. The purpose... to do the work you love, to do what you believe is right, to be the best father for your child, to be the best spouse for your love, to help others rise up in the world, and to care for each other.

These sound like clichés, and you might say, "Well… everyone wants to do that". Yes, they do! But they choose not to because that's not what we believe is our purpose. We have been somewhat blinded. Our hearts speak to us about them, but they have lost their value and meaning. We no longer believe our hearts, or just simply become afraid of our dreams.

We all have gotten our hearts broken at one time or another. As I stated earlier, life tends to make us afraid of change. It keeps us from the possibility of getting hurt. Our brain wants to keep us safe. After several bad experiences, your brain tells you "okay, that made you feel sad, let's not experience those feelings anymore". So it uses fear to keep you from change, from expressing yourself too much, from feeling and loving too much. It keeps you away from the edge. It does not want you to feel scared, yet it uses fear to actually scare you away from fear itself. When we no longer feel the Edge of love and become too scared to get close to the Edge of fear, it becomes very hard to see our purpose. We must listen to our heart and do the things that bring us fear and discomfort. When we practice walking alongside the Edge of fear, we start to discover our purpose. Don't be afraid to follow your heart, to love openly, to do the work that you love and to fight for what you believe is right. This leads us to our purpose. It will lead you in a way that you won't even notice in the beginning that you have found your purpose. You'll be in the middle of practicing your craft, and all of sudden, you'll realize, "wow, my heart feels right!". That uneasy feeling you've had in your chest, will no longer be there. We might become like our young old selves. We start to live our lives with more passion and a sense of purpose. The catch is that we must trust that our hearts and our strengths will get us to our purpose.

We cannot just do this sitting in the comfort of our current states. We must be willing to face fear. We must open up ourselves and be willing to follow what our heart tells us. We must trust ourselves and constantly take action and face our fears.

Looking backwards and walking

Fear tends to build up in our minds; everything bad that has happened to us affects how we look at ourselves and how resistant we are to change. We get caught in our pasts. Our hearts tell us what we should be doing, what our calling is, but fear has kept us in the past. Our fear keeps us from moving forward. We try to stay away from everything that scares us or requires change. Your heart doesn't lie to you, though. It keeps reminding you to follow it. The problem is that you're stuck – you're not moving forward until you get close to the Edge of fear and face it.

Many people are stuck in the past in one way or another. Some of us are wishing things would be like before, or judge ourselves based on the past. We may develop our own standard for life based on our past. It's like as if we're trying to walk forward as we look behind us. Imagine walking down a path where you could never turn around and go backwards: you can only turn left or right as you move forward, and then you're passing a beautiful field of flowers, but as you continue walking, the path is no longer lined by flower fields so we look back at the field, and yet walk forward. As we look back, we then miss out on the beauty and opportunity that lie in front of us. When we do notice those paths that lead to other beautiful places, we will have already passed them. When we do notice them, they will already be behind us and it becomes too late to turn towards them. So many of us are so caught up with holding on to the past that we lose sight of the opportunities in front of us. It's never too late, though, to turn your head and walk along the path of life facing forward.

We must strive to experience our lives while always looking forward. Though, it's true that sometimes we won't be walking along a path of flowers and will be walking through a scary, dark forest instead. We will still see the beauty that lies ahead of us, however, and will be able to turn into those paths that lead us there. We will experience more this way than constantly living a life looking back at our past lives, and thus measuring ourselves based on that view.

We all remember that lonely kid in school we thought was odd and quiet. Take, for example, a man we'll call "Barry". He grew up getting good grades in school, but had extreme social interaction difficulties and therefore didn't have many friends. Deep down every child wants a friend, as many studies have shown, that having good relationships with peers is one of the essential elements for the development of self-esteem, happiness and overall success in the world. Yet, Barry and other's around him had no idea that he essentially had a social learning difficulty, which is why Social Skills classes should be required courses early on during childhood and in high school. We should not expect all children to simply learn social skills on their own, some have to be taught. Just like we are all born with innate strengths and weakness in abilities such as language, attention and memory, some children are born with innate social competencies too, which can negatively impact their life. Barry was judged solely on what others saw. He saw this perception of how he was viewed, and over time, identified with it, thinking... "You know, maybe I'm just not a social person, I can't have any friends, and I'm only good at school." He lived his life based on his own judgment of the kind of person who he was. He didn't play sports because his parents didn't have the time to pick him up from practice. He lived a life that was set up for him. He didn't have control of these kinds of factors. It's very hard to realize this is happening when you're young. Many times we just blame ourselves and believe that those things are happening to us because that's just how we are. Barry constantly played out this idea of his past self and lived his life based on those assumptions. 'I can't make friends, I don't like to dance, I don't like to interact with other cultures, I don't like to go out to downtown, I don't like to speak in front of others, I can't be successful. These are all assumptions based on our pasts.

We are looking backwards, we are not present, and we can't see the beauty and love in front of us. It becomes very difficult for Barry, as an adult, to try and get out of his head and overcome his social skills difficulty. It becomes hard for him to be fit; "I'm just not an athletic person," he says to himself. "I can't take that position because it's going to require speaking in front of others". "I can't ask that person out, because I'm just not very attractive". Most of this is based on fear of the past and overcoming some past difficulties. Fear of experiencing ourselves in a different way. Barry feels safe now, and he's hurt less often because he stays away from the fear of having to interact with the world around him because of the hurt that he has experienced by society. He doesn't do the things that might scare him, the things that give him an uneasy feeling in his chest. He keeps his heart closed, to protect himself from relieving those negative memories etched by society.

I was lucky to have an experience so that, now that I look back, I understand this concept better. When I first migrated to the U.S., I came here not knowing English. I knew basic words like 'hello' and 'sit', but that was it. To make it even more difficult, I entered 5th grade in November. Everyone had already met their friends, everyone had their cliques, and there was me on my own. A little Spanish kid from Venezuela who had just left everything he knew to come to a whole new place. The first students who gravitated towards me were the "bad kids". They would ask me to say cuss words in the middle of class, and with me not knowing their meanings, I would say them. The kids would all laugh and I thought it was great to be part of their group. Meanwhile, Mrs. Smalls would sit me outside of class as punishment. I now look back and understand why these kids gravitated towards me. I was an easy target, I was easily moldable, and so they could make me into whatever they wanted me to be. I didn't have knowledge of the new culture I was in and I didn't know the language. Since I was in ESOL (English for speakers of other languages) I had to have lunch with all the ESOL kids and couldn't have lunch with the rest of my classmates. In ESOL, there were a lot of kids like me, who had just moved from a different country, and whose families had very little money, and I would sometimes run into them at the thrift stores. A lot of them, like me, hung out with the bad kids. When you enter school as a kid who doesn't know a countries language, It's very hard to be selective about your friends or your environment. Negative groups or people, want to influence others to justify their views or behavior and anyone can join. That's why I tended to be around those people during school. Now when I look back, I see there was one specific event that woke me up. It made me realize the path I was going along and where I was going to end up.

It started with my 7th grade math teacher, Mrs. Rosaria Wills. She was this strong, little Italian lady from Florence, Italy. The kind of woman you just don't want to mess with, and she always told it like it is. One day, I got in trouble in her class because I was horsing around with the bad kids in the middle of class. Afterwards, she asked me to stay and help her clean the board as punishment. I remember that it was just her and I in the classroom, in complete silence. I started to clean the board as she graded papers. Out of the blue, she said, "Carlos, why do you see yourself in that way?" I was confused. I didn't know what she meant. "Hang out with them and not see your potential…." "You are better than those kids think you are; I see it in you, I know that's not you, that's how you see yourself because you are limited. You have one of the best grades in my class for tests, but choose not to do your homework like the people you hang out with." I asked her what she meant by my being limited. "You are limited because you are only seeing the bad – they are taking you down the ugly path and you are walking on it because that's the only thing you know." Her voice slowly got louder and angrier, and I will always remember what she said next. "Promise me something right now – you are going to try and make one new friend that doesn't hang out with that group." And in an awkward reply, I said 'yes'.

I ended up missing my bus home after class, so I called home and no one picked up. My mom usually worked late and I always relied on the bus to take me home. So I began walking. During the walk, I thought about what my teacher had said. It hit my heart, as I understood what was going on, but the thought of making new friends and being somebody new scared me.

That night, I was lying in bed when I heard the door open, and knew it was my mom. I saw her through the cracked door… tired, beaten down, sitting down to have dinner by herself at the table, as everyone was already sleeping. I could feel her heart, I could feel her struggle, I could feel her cry and her optimism to get us out of the bad situation we were in. All of a sudden, I started to relive the memory of when my father took my brother and I inside the plane and put our seat belts on, and said goodbye when we left Venezuela. I could see his saddened face as he held back the tears and told us to always listen to my mom and protect each other. I understood the bigger picture better, and I understand it even more today. As I saw my mother eat the left-over dinner, tears rolled down my face. Even to this day, as I remember that life-changing moment and as I write this, tears roll down my face. It was a beautiful moment of realization and growth because of the love I have for my parents. During that moment, I realized I was not doing anything to honor their sacrifice to give us a better life and their pain. I felt I was dishonoring them and disrespecting them. I was letting my past and the circumstances around me dictate my life. That night, I grew up a lot. I realized that I had to stop being friends with the bad kids. They didn't want me to succeed or become better than them. Many of my friends at the time were poor, in the same situation I was in. Mothers, working at cleaning hotel rooms, fathers delivering pizza or working in restaurants. My mom drove a beat up 86' Celica and worked two jobs. One job cleaning hotel rooms during the day and one at a retail clothing store at night. My step dad drove an 87' Volvo that I later drove for a bit in high school, and he worked at a computer warehouse and would deliver pizzas at night. I thought to myself that, in order to help them, I had to be different. I had to stop measuring myself by the past and my environment. I had to look for opportunities to become better so I could help and honor my parents' sacrifice to give us a better chance at life. After all, we were a family and I had to do my part.

The next day, I was so emotionally moved that I completely avoided my existing friends. I hated who I had become, and hated them for what they'd done to me. When I was saying cuss words in class, not knowing their meaning, they were just laughing at me. I hated myself for being treated like a mockery or used as entertainment, because I'd been too content thinking others liked me. I'd never had the chance to choose my path. I'd just let other people and circumstances dictate my life and what I was capable of. Just like it happened to me, this is what happens to us in different ways and various aspects of our lives. We are blinded by our past circumstances, by what society tells us that we are; we measure ourselves with a short ruler or by other peoples' rulers. We essentially go through life not looking forward. We are fearful of change so we choose to remain where we are at. We somehow trick ourselves into thinking that is who we were meant to be, and we are not seeing the opportunities around us because we are stuck on a certain perception we believe of our current lives. We are essentially walking on the path of life, looking backwards.

When I did decide to change and get away from the corrupt kids, I felt very alone. I got a lot of backlash when they saw me hanging out with new people. I got called all sorts of names by my old friends who were suddenly hateful towards me. I got picked on by the very same people who used to be my friends. I started to make new friends, though, and as a result, I started to behave differently.

One of the first people who I met was Pete. I remember going over to his house the first time. He lived in a nice neighborhood, and his parents were very welcoming and treated me with respect. I got to see a different side of life. I was actually able to play in a real neighborhood, do things I'd never gotten to do before; then I met my friend Mark, who even to this day I'm still great friends with. He was always pushing to be better at soccer and we would go practice after school on our own. I got to see a different mindset in people. Then, as time progressed, the quality of people who I became friends with changed my life for the better and I started following my own heart. I embraced my difference, but also became stronger because I was able to change the course that my life had taken before. I faced a lot of fears during that transition period and changing the perception I had of life, but I became better at letting go of the resistance I had to change due to fear. I understood the bigger picture a little better. This is what we must do – listen to our heart and don't be afraid to follow what it's telling us. When we decide to follow our heart and feel closer to the edges of our lives, we will face many fears, but understand that this is part of the overall process of growing and facing life head-on.

Shining Beacon to The Edge

If we look back at history, we'll see that people have achieved unimaginable feats. They were able to conquer things that were greater than them. When the only person that believed in them was themselves, and when everyone told them that it was impossible. This is one of the reasons why I love reading biographies of great men and women who have taken something that didn't exist and brought it to the world. The innovators of every time period. The invention of the wheel, the invention of flight, harnessing the power of electricity... one person starting a movement and changing the world because of their sole belief – and heart – put into a cause. People like Thomas Edison, Henry Ford, Martin Luther King, Jr., Mohammed Ghandi, Simon Bolivar, Elon Musk and Jeff Bezos.

Their stories are great examples of following your heart and mind. They are the extremes, the outer edges, and an example of how close one can get to a personal edge if you truly live your life by seeking your edges. Each one of them represents a different edge and gives you glimpses of how close to the edge one can really get. They all encountered great amounts of fear and periods of disbelief in themselves, but they all continued forward in achieving what they believed in, despite being in hostile and insecure places. I like to look at them as the examples of what's possible when you are determined to follow your heart and seek the edges of life. They asked questions. How much faster can I get this car to go? How many more people can I feed? How big can I get my start-up? How much better can I make this surgical procedure? How good of a friend can I be? How much can I actually love? And, How close can I actually really get to that edge?

These are some of the questions that our hearts ask our minds. Many of us, though, choose not to listen and act. We get lost in the static of the world that we live in. It's such a busy world, with countless distractions and entertainments. We tend to work longer hours in corporate America than ever before. We have been exposed to the most marketing ever in human history. Things are constantly calling our minds for attention. When our heart tries to speak amidst all of the noise, it becomes very hard to hear. It can become so extreme that some eventually stop being able to hear their hearts ever again, until they are in the silence of their deathbed, and by then, their path might have ended. These individuals represent the other extreme. The greats have followed their edges, when compared to those who got lost in the static noise of life, and they show us what the two extremes are when you refuse to face your fears versus following your heart.

We then can use these examples as bearings to guide us on the correct paths. That's what we must find first. Look for examples of those edges that others have gone to, and use that to follow on the path of that edge… and after you reach that edge, you decide to get closer and become a beacon for the next person looking for that specific edge.

I love the phrase, "Seek and you shall find". I strongly believe in this: if you really seek something, you will tend to find it. Whether getting too close to that edge impacts your life negatively or positively, if you consistently seek it, you will eventually find it. If you believe in a cause, you will eventually find somebody else who feels like you or someone that will believe in you. If you seek true love, day in and day out, you will eventually be surrounded by it. Everything in our world that has been new, innovative, and life-changing was always impossible. Records are broken all the time, dreams are achieved every day, love is felt everywhere. Anything is possible, but we must first begin to follow our hearts and fight our fears.

What does your heart tell you about certain aspects of your life? Take time to feel it, take time to understand why it makes your heart race, or why it brings about fear. Many of us don't tune out the world and speak to our hearts. Take time out of your day, to be alone and have an honest conversation with your heart. People used to make fun of Thomas Edison because he used to go into an empty room with nothing but a chair and a desk to think. Seek and feel for your own edges, take time to get to know yourself, and your journey there will be clearer, despite the darkness around you.

One Last Thing About Fear..

Fear, is experienced in many different ways according to the life you live. Some of us are scared to ride a bicycle and some of us are fearful of talking to a crowd of 20 people. Our standards of fear are different, but for most of us who decide to follow our hearts and feel the edges, it starts out as small fears that all add up to one big reason not to do something. This can be the fear of going to the gym to lose weight because people will judge you, or fearing a change in your diet with the thought that food will no longer taste good. The fear of thinking differently from everyone else, for the fear that people will not understand you. Many of these fears are created by your mind to keep you safe and keep you from experiencing pain. Fears, sometimes, are past experiences that you fear might happen again, and therefore you stay away from following your heart because you might experience that pain again.

Fear comes in all shapes and sizes, but you must remember that fear cannot stop you physically – it can only stop you mentally. You have the option to move past fear, regardless of the size of it. Even though there are many types of fears, there's only one way to conquer it, and that is to decide to move forward. It makes fear this neutral thing that you must learn to always face. As you face your small fears, they will prepare you to conquer bigger ones. That is why it's important you start with even the smallest of fears. Every time you conquer even the smallest of fears, right then and there, you grow a little more, you become a little better, you trust your heart more, and you feel the edges more closely. This is how facing our fears develops us. It doesn't completely change us or make us better overnight, but it does accomplish these feats, the more we push past it. That's why we must face even the smallest of fears that keep us from following our hearts.

Part Four- Action: The Key To Accomplishing Our Journey

"You can't cross the sea merely by standing and staring at the water."
-Rabindranath Tagore

We have developed greatly when it comes to human innovation, but we have distanced ourselves from who we truly are and our connectedness to the world around us. We all feel the call of our hearts to come closer to the edges and follow our hearts at some point in our lives. The static noise has become louder and louder; it has become harder and harder to listen to our hearts. We have so many distractions and so many demands that we no longer have time to give our hearts the time to speak.

Our hearts' calls are for us to go the edges. To translate the beauty of the universe by getting as close to the Edge of love as we can. Fear overtakes our minds or we simply become indifferent to the world. We shut down in desperation to avoid fear. Many of us have become complacent with our lives so that we no longer see the color in life. We have let fear confuse us into thinking we can't be great. It has lied to us, as to what greatness is and the only people who can achieve it. Fear is the biggest liar of the world. It talks to you in a convincing way, but when it can no longer convince you, it speaks with panic.

As we've learned, fear keeps us away from the edge. It does that to protect you from emotional harm. When your heart calls you, fear stands in front of your path and tells you not to go on because the path is dark and uncertain. As you stand in front of it, seeing the dim light at the end of the path in your mind, there's that determining split moment where you decide to either keep walking past fear or remain frozen in fear and indecision, where you don't walk forward. If you think about it, even a simple random event can change your whole life forever. Imagine how much we affect our own lives through a decision like this, to move past fear. It's very powerful because you are in control; you are the decision maker in that moment. It's not a random event – it's you making a decision. It's your Edge of courage, and belief, and your love which are tested in that moment. It's the split second where we have to take the first step and take action. Imagine how our lives could be if we lived our lives, listening and following our heart, rather than letting random events dictate certain aspects of our lives because we are frozen in fear, too frozen to follow our heart and feel for our edges. Feel the person that you can really be. The change you can really make. The love you can really give and the gifts you can leave to the world, no matter how big or small.

You have the ability to make a positive impact on the world around you. I have witnessed how one doctor can impact a whole surgery department, thus impacting the surgery staff around him and the patients obtaining better treatment, thus impacting the community around that hospital and the quality of people's lives. All this, potentially, because of a doctor's attitude towards his staff and patients. Many times, we don't know the impact we have on people's lives, and even more if we think on to the ones who we never meet. This is how every single one of us can impact the world around us. By impacting our children, those we work with, and our quality of life.

We do this by setting an example for others, showing that it is okay to seek our edges and listen to our heart. In order to do this, though, we must walk past fear and we must take proactive action... and begin to walk in the paths that our hearts tells us. We have to trust that getting there will get us closer to feeling our edges and our lives more closely.

Before the Action

As you sit and contemplate whether to take action and begin moving forward, you must take time to listen to your heart. Feel the fear, understand why you are feeling the fear, and accept it. Really take time out of your day to think about what your heart says. What do you want to do? What do you want to build? Who do you want to help? Or, who do you want to love? Listen to yourself deeply.

I never thought I would ever sit and meditate, but it helps greatly to quiet the noise around you. The first time I tried to meditate, it was very awkward, I felt out of place and strange. Fear was kicking in full throttle and my mind was racing with thoughts, but as I began to focus on my breathing and the feeling of letting go, it became very empowering. It becomes easier to open up and listen to your heart. Meditation trains us to be more in our mind, and to strengthen our focus.

The first couple times I meditated I felt very out of control because my focus kept wandering away from my breathing and became very frustrating. I could barely sit for a couple minutes and stay focused on my breathing while my eyes were closed. My brain was begging for some external stimuli to distract me from my breathing. Many of us have a hard time actually controlling our breathing throughout the day. We let our minds just breathe, based on how we're feeling in any given moment. Some of us go through the day with constant anxiety, where we breathe very little. Some of us can be enormously stressed, and breathe by taking short breaths, and also don't breathe normally. How we breathe controls how our body biologically responds to stressors and the disturbances around us.. In order to listen to your heart, you have to quiet the noise around you and you must begin with the closest disturbance… and that is yourself. Meditation teaches you to breathe slower and deeper. This is the natural breath.

We must learn to take time during the day to be conscious of our breathing. When we meditate, the disturbing static noise quiets down and the world moves a little slower. You feel in the present slightly more than before. You notice the world around you a bit differently. It is a tool that we can learn to use to control the static noise around us. The basics of meditation are to focus on your breathing as you sit in a quiet place. Don't force yourself to stop thinking your normal thoughts; just focus on your breathing, slow and deep, and eventually the talking in your mind will quiet down. Fear will try to take you out of focus as you're doing something that you've never done before. The talking will begin, but as you focus on your breathing, it will again subside. Try to do this at least five minutes out of your day, and you will eventually find yourself meditating for longer periods of time.

Get involved with meditation even if it's just 5-10 minutes out of your day. Try to quiet down your mind and speak to your heart. Even if you have to go for a run or a walk, alone. You can still quiet your mind as you do a physical activity. Get in your zone and listen to your heart. It becomes harder to feel your edges when you don't know where they actually are... until you learn to listen to your heart. Give yourself the time to meditate.

Once you know which edges you want to move towards, it will be easier to find where those paths are located. Once you find your way there and fear is standing on your path, you can then take action.

Action and Fear

In order to know you're taking action in finding what you believe your edges are, you must be moving towards fear. I hear people say, "I just don't know what to do with myself, or what my purpose is". Start with taking actions towards your fears. If you have a fear of not traveling because you've never traveled abroad, book that trip. If you're afraid to start jogging because you can't jog, start walking. If you are afraid to follow your passion because you're afraid you won't make as much money as you have in the past, start doing it on the side while working your regular job.

It's all about doing the small things that scare you, but which your heart craves, as long as they positively impact your life or the lives of others. Your heart will speak love, so listen to the things it says. Start by taking action toward the things that your heart says you should do, and yet you choose not to because of excuses or fear. Write down your goals or the changes you want to make and keep them in your purse or wallet. Read them every day. These are your edges that you are seeking: you have to know where they are located so that you can take correct action and follow the path to get there.

Jot down a map of a couple of ways you can take to start getting closer to feeling those edges. An action that you can start taking to get closer to that edge that you seek. Write these actions on a to-do list so you can refer to them daily and work on them. These serve as your map during your life journey. What action or direction can you take to get closer to the light at the end of the path? We are easily distracted, so we need constant reminders of the actions we need to take to get closer to our goals and dreams. When you're shaken by fear or by the world around you, keep walking and believe in your heart.

Map Your Path

As I sat in my office staring at my computer, I knew I had to find my purpose and feel my edges. I felt disconnected from life. I knew I had to face my fears and follow my heart, but I didn't know where to start. As I read self-help books and attended seminars, I got motivated to reach for my edges, but when it came down to it, I got lost in the noise.

Do you ever find yourself starting something, and then you all of a sudden stop? We think that what we're doing is not big enough, that our actions are too small. Yet, everyone has to start somewhere, and we all have the power to do it. We have to work with what we have. We have to be realistic and begin moving on our paths with the tools at hand. Many of us sit and wish we had a better opportunity, a better economy, a better situation, or that opportunity that comes out of the blue. This fear and indecision is what stops most people.

Our fear makes up excuses to keep us from walking in the path that our hearts lay before us. Its main job is to develop doubt in us so that we can turn back. It wants to keep us away from the edges. "You're not ready to tackle this change, you're not capable of doing that, you can try and learn, but you're not really going to succeed." These are some of the excuses our minds create. In order to take action, you must first chart your course of action.

Thor Heyerdahl was a Norwegian writer and explorer who is most famously known for his five thousand mile voyage across the

Pacific Ocean from South America to the Toamotu Islands in a hand-constructed wooden raft in 1947. Thor Heyerdahl theorized that ancient people could travel long voyages across the ocean and come in contact with other cultures thousands of miles away. Scholars had always believed that Polynesia was eventually settled by those traveling from the West (Africa) since this option was closer to Africa and had less open water requiring travel, but Heyerdahl believed that it had been settled by ancient travelers from South America (farther away and requiring that more open water be traversed). He found archeological evidence while living in Polynesia, and this pointed out clues to communication between people of South America and Polynesia. When he brought his findings to other scholars and scientific organizations around the world, he was ridiculed. Many of his colleagues started treating him as an outsider and a sham.

He felt very lost and helpless. Nobody at that time wanted to give him the time of day to hear about his theories. He felt very frustrated, because he believed deep in his heart that ancient people of South America had traveled across the Pacific Ocean to reach Polynesia. He had no idea where to even begin to prove this, however, after most of the scientific community laughed at him and nobody took him seriously. So, he thought, "what can I do right now, to prove this to the rest of the world?".

He realized the only thing that was available to him at the time was the Pacific Ocean itself. The same natural materials that the ancients had used to travel were still there. Making a bold move and following his heart, he decided he was going to travel to South America and build a replica of the same type of raft which would have been used, one built by the same native natural resources there, and sail to Polynesia to prove his theory. One would think somebody like this was insane, to go to these lengths to prove what he believed was right and give credit to a people that were long forgotten. He wasn't insane, though; his heart was calling him onto the path to reach that edge, and only fear was standing in the way, telling him he was crazy to take on such a great feat... yet he pushed on. He made contact with those he knew to raise money, he contacted men he knew to go along on the journey with him, and he received help from the U.S. Army in exchange for information about the ocean and rations.

Can you imagine the fear he felt as he sailed off in a wooden raft to take on a journey spanning five thousand miles across an ocean, with only the faith in himself that his theory about ocean and wind currents were correct? He also had to uphold his word to the other five men who trusted their lives with him. The fear must have been immense, and yet he pushed on. He charted a course and started with what he had available to him at the time. Eventually, after much hardship and traveling for one hundred and one days, they reached one of the neighboring islands of Toamotu, proving his theory correct.

Thor Heyerdahl would have not been able to accomplish all of this if he hadn't had his idea mapped out. He could have easily stopped listening to his heart and forgotten about his theory and go along with what was scientifically correct at the time and avoid ridicule, but he created a plan of action and executed it with courage and belief in himself. Just like Thor, we all need a written plan that we can always look to when we are wondering what action to take next.

You must take time for yourself and write down all the edges you want to feel. Do you want to be a better parent? Do you want to change the culture of your company? Do you want to follow your heart? Do you want to raise your standard of living? Do you want to be fit again? Do you want to love the world around you better? Figure out what edges you want to feel and make them clear to you, to the point where you don't have to constantly take time to figure out what they are. Write them down so you can read them when you wake up and when you go to bed. It sounds repetitive and crazy, but it's what we must do if we want to remain on the path towards those points where our hearts call us to go.

Our Limitations

As we sit alone and listen to our hearts, many questions arise when we decide to move forward and strive for the things that call us. Fear starts to make excuses according to our beliefs and limitations. Regardless of what your limitation is, your beliefs are set according to what you think is possible. Our limitations dictate our actions. They set us up so that a janitor's belief in the possibility that he will become a Fortune 500 CEO is lower, incomparable to others, such as someone like a Harvard Business graduate. It's all because of the limitations our minds and fears set for us. Now, maybe the janitor I've mentioned grew up in circumstances that make this achievement seemingly impossible, but if that's what his heart has called on him to accomplish, he can likely surpass his limitations and achieve the goal which he once thought impossible . We are all born with the same physical abilities to love and the ability to listen to our hearts. It is up to us to follow them and fight the limitations that keep us from seeking our paths to feel the edges. We are all limited by our beliefs and assumptions.

This is why goal setting and achievement is so important. It allows us to move forward by experiencing life at a higher level. Before you take action, take time to listen to your heart and write your goals down. This allows you to see them every day and envision them. Anything that was ever accomplished first had a vision. If we are so busy with our daily lives, just simply trying to survive on a daily basis, it becomes extremely trying to follow our hearts. When our goal is simply to get through our day, there's very little thinking involved in what we want for our futures. It leaves very little energy for our inspiration and imagination. Many of us are simply too busy with our daily lives to step out of the societal train and take time to envision what our hearts want.

I believe that the reason poverty and wars exist is because there's not enough listening to our hearts being done; many of us and especially those in power are not feeling for the edges of compassion and understanding of the big picture, let alone the purposes we have in life. Your current circumstances are your current circumstances. We all have them in different ways, but we must be mindful to take time and listen to what our hearts say to us. Some of us, especially people who are in very difficult situations, such as poverty or oppression where they can't even afford the luxury of thinking about the big picture of the universe and truly following their heart, are limited greatly such as in famine/war stricken countries For those that do have the luxury to seek thought outside of simply trying to survive everyday life, for many of us, the fear and the ability to step out of the current societal train and following our hearts, have kept our universal consciousness from expanding. It is a constant battle we face every day on whether we go along with the masses or stay true to ourselves, thus dictating if we are indeed following our hearts. Therefore, for many of us it's simply easier to go along with the crowd and putting the edges our hearts calls on us to seek on hold.

Becoming aware of which edges you want to seek, and listening to your heart will serve as a constant vision. Once you create a vision, you open up the very unique possibility of bringing it to life. If we think in the simplest term for what a thought is, whether that is energy, matter or some other unexplained reason. In order to produce a thought, which would involve neuron to neuron communication, it would require a form of energy in order to create that impulse or communication between the two neurons, we can then say, that a thought is essentially a transfer of energy or an event that required a transfer of energy in order for it to happen. Thus that specific transfer of energy which now became a thought is essentially a form of energy if we rely on Newtonian theory. In a sense, it is now made to exist and it is up to you to bring it to life if that's what you truly desire. Like Issac Newton's theory of energy, that energy cannot be created nor destroyed; it can only be transferred. Your thoughts are energy. Everything in the world is made up of energy. When those visions are created in your mind, they cannot be destroyed; they can only be transferred. It can sit in your mind for all of your life and never be transferred into another form of energy that the world can feel, touch, or see. It remains in your mind, with fear as the gate keeper, to inhibit you from following your chosen path, and keeping you from transferring it into the physical world as another form of energy that can be experienced by others. Instead, we must write our goals down and envision them every day as we begin to take action and start walking on the path our hearts have signaled for us.

As you conquer each leg of your journey, the limited ceiling above you will get higher and you will grow as the belief in yourself and the vision of seeing yourself accomplishing the goals that you wrote and envisioned before you propel you forward. This causes you to grow mentally and expand your consciousness as you get closer to feeling your edges. This is why they must be written and reviewed daily, to serve as a path and increase your belief in what you can actually accomplish by moving closer to your edges.

I love the story of Roger Banister. He is a true example of how one person can change others' limitations, simply by accomplishing something that others thought was impossible. Doctors and scientists at that time said that it was impossible for humans to run faster than a 4 minute mile. Somehow, before Roger Banister, nobody had broken that record. Everyone thought it was never going to happen, and yet he did it. Forty-six days after Banister broke the record, someone else broke the four minute record, and many men since then have broken the four minute mile record. By seeing the vision of himself breaking the four minute record, he created the very possibility of it happening in the world. As he practiced day in and day out, with the belief that it was possible, and knowing the vision at the end of the path, he was able to transfer that energy that he had in his mind and release it into the world. He showed the world that it was possible, and the limitations were lowered. He fought against doubt and fear, but as he was running and crossing the mile finish mark, in that specific snapshot in time, he felt his edges of his life. It's a moment that you work for with nothing, but belief in your heart, and when you reach it, you move the bar of possibility a little higher and change history forever.

Ayrton Senna, one the best formula one race car drivers in the world, broke many records during his career.. He would say that there were certain times during a race where he felt completely in the present, almost as if God was driving the car, and during those moments, announcers would say that he pushed his car to the outer edges of its limits, almost as if the car was taking corners with half of the back wheels on the outer edge of the track. When you look at footage, of Senna racing– during his turns – it looks as if he was almost able to bend the car around a corner. He said there were times where he would just cry after a race, after the feeling he experienced; he described it as feeling as if God was there with him. Senna lived his life by constantly feeling the edges of life. He started children's foundations to help the poor that, even to this day, still help millions in Brazil. He was involved in many hobbies and constantly pushed himself to be a better person to those around him. People loved him because of the energy that he would give out. All the thoughts that came from his heart – he would push to transfer them into the physical world, either by driving a formula one car like nobody had ever driven before, or by impacting those around him in the most positive way possible.

Senna broke many limits for people. During his racing career, Brazil was going through a very difficult time of poverty and injustice. For people then, Senna was an inspiration, and he still is to this day. He allowed those who watched him to see where the edges of love, action, passion, grit, and tenacity laid. He gave people glimpses of the edges, and just like Roger Banister helped others feel their edges. Senna was able to give people a sense of direction and a sense of purpose. Each one of them changed the universal consciousness. They were men of action who took on many fearful journeys for the purpose of following their hearts and to getting closer to their edges. They both had a sense of urgency to transfer their thoughts and beliefs into the physical world. Whether it was the thought and belief that a record could be broken, or pushing themselves to the outer limits because of something or someone they loved. In order to start your journey, you have to be aware that you sometimes must see past your limits or current state. The moment you begin any journey to follow your heart, you become more in control of your life as you take action and walk your path every day. The past no longer matters; just the present moment is involved as you build the future.

When you get rid of some of your limits and look past them, It frees you and makes it easier to stay the course. Keep track of your goals and set goals that are above your limits. Get in the habit of dreaming above your limits, and conquer them. Love more. Care more. Believe in yourself more, because as long you are doing something positive for the world, even in the smallest of ways, you are serving your purpose to the universe by creating and feeling the love around you. Inherently feeling the edges that life has to offer.

First Thing in the Morning

As you wake up each morning to begin your new day, the easiest way to begin your journey towards the edges is to wake up earlier. Now, I use to hear this all the time that all successful people woke up early, that the rich wake up earlier than everyone else, which is just not always true. Waking up early though affects your life positively when you feel you don't have any time during the day to do those things in which your heart calls on you for. This was one of the biggest game changers for me personally. It's something simple, and an action through which you can see positive changes in your day. Many of us wake up to an alarm clock, brush our teeth, drink our coffee, eat breakfast or drink a shake, and in a hurry, head out the door, fight traffic, work, leave work to fight traffic, get home, shower, eat dinner, watch tv, sleep, and repeat. Where in that time of day was there any time for you to be able to listen to your heart, let alone work to follow it?

Waking up earlier was the x factor that I credit towards propelling my life forward and allowing me to gain more control of it. It's so easy to just sit in the ocean and let the current dictate where your boat is going to go for the day. This is what happens to us. We don't have a charted course for the day. We rely on created patterns/currents that steer our lives/boats and give us an illusion that we are going somewhere, and every now and then, we hit an island.

Be like a ship captain: chart your course the night before and wake up early to go over the course you will take for that day. This prevents you from getting lost in the noise, and it gives you the time to actually have a plan for that day, of where you are intending to go. You turn on the engines and you steer the boat in the direction you choose. You refuse to only let the currents of life dictate where you will end up in your life's journey.

When we are asked to make changes to our regular habits, in order to really change, we must focus on one specific part of the change and must be able to feel the difference it makes in our lives, and we must actually like it. This is where I think some personal development books fail. They ask us to make changes which all have good intentions for the reader, and are delivered well, but the reader/listener becomes overwhelmed, and many times, doesn't really continue on with taking action because they don't feel the change right away. Many times, it makes you feel bad about yourself because you think that you must be different than the ideal person the author talks about in the book, and that you are a failure for not being successful or not waking up early to go over your goals in the morning. In order to keep applying myself and follow my heart to feel my edges, I started moving in baby steps. I started with one habit I wanted to change in my day, and would do that for a couple of days; then I added one more thing, like writing my goals for the next day before I went to sleep, and did that for a couple of weeks; then I added another change, like meditating for at least five minutes during my day and quieting my mind. Once I embraced and accepted each change, and witnessed the positive change it was making in my life, then I slowly added more changes to my previous habits. You have to become comfortable with the given change before you make more because then you forget about the previous ones and essentially can feel overwhelmed because let's face it, changing our behavior can be hard.

Start by getting up thirty minutes earlier than your normal time. Do everything you normally do, and then at the end of the day, ask yourself how you felt throughout your day. Were you more relaxed? Did the world slow down a bit? At any point, did you hear your heart speak? Did you feel a bit more in control?

Ask yourself these questions. Just like you get to know your fears, you must get to know your change. When you made the decision to get up early that day, you automatically became more in control of your life. Most of our lives' schedules are prewritten by our jobs and families. This is not a bad thing: it's just life. By just deciding to take ownership of those thirty minutes, though, you become more in control of your life's schedule. Because you got up earlier, you had time to cook a healthier breakfast that you prefer instead of eating what your schedule generally allows. Because you had more time in your morning, you might have left earlier and not felt rushed during morning traffic, and been less stressed. Because you got up earlier, maybe you had time to take your lunch in the park outside of your office and you met the love of your life as a result of that, or you simply heard your heart speak. Because you got up earlier, you might have had some time to listen to your kid or notice your wife's or husband's love. In order to get closer to our edges, we must take back some of the control that daily life has imposed on us.

After you've felt this edge, now walk closer to it and get up an hour earlier next time, and then ask yourself those questions again. This time, though, since you have extra time, take five minutes out of your morning and sit quietly, and think about the things you are thankful for. You're going to feel resistance, but just say them anyway. During all these changes you make to your daily habits, oftentimes your fear will speak to you. "This is stupid, this is not going to do anything for me. Why am I doing things that a book is telling me to do? I should know what to do." This is all part of it. Constantly keep seeking your edges of what you can accomplish by having extra time in your day. Next time, write your goals the night before and go over them during that time. By writing your goals down, you begin to set them in motion in your mind, thus causing your mind to seek the actions you must take to accomplish them during your day. It helps to have time to ourselves in the morning because this allows us to take time, to listen to our hearts and visit our fears.

What Really Works

Before I continue talking about the things that I believe in, and which have worked for me in my journey to feel the edges of my personal development, I want to remind you of one thing. When I decided to write this book, I wanted to focus more on letting you, the reader, take what I say and make your own decisions. I want you to interpret my words as my experience with life, and as what I believe is true. As I sit here writing, I am always speaking from the heart. In moments where I feel I'm not fully able to translate what is in my heart to you, I stop and dig deeper until I can. I wanted to speak to you as if I was speaking to my brother or future children. I know that we might be far or near, but I wrote this with the intention of getting you closer to your heart. Whichever way that might be, you're the only one who can listen to it; therefore, listen to my words by interpreting them according to what speaks to your edges, and to your life.

We all want to know the things that work, the sure thing, the magic recipe and the magic steps that are going to change our lives for the better. I've learned that there is not one specific action that can do all of this. We must work on first taking action and putting ourselves out there to try different methods which work for us in order to begin our journeys to get closer to our edges. The habits and actions I describe are things that have worked for me. They created a positive change in my daily life. I never learned them growing up, though I feel there should be required courses in high school and college to wake up our hearts. Unfortunately, our education system has failed us in one of the most important parts of the human experience. These are the habits and thinking I've followed to get closer to my heart and seek my edges. Therefore, don't stop seeking other ways to bring you closer to them. Don't just take what I say for granted; try it and see for yourself if my suggestions make a positive difference in your life. But don't just believe or disbelieve anything I say. Really try it out, and start with the thoughts that speak to you the most.

There are many great mentors out there who can each change someone's life in a positive way through their respective messages. Each one of them has a different experience and different story that you might strongly relate to. I hope that some of my stories and experiences speak to you, but don't stop learning about yourself, and read about other people's takes on life. Take everything that you learn and choose the tools available to carve the masterpiece that is your life.

Writing Dreams Down

Imagine going to the store to buy your weekly groceries. Is it faster and more efficient when you go there with a list of everything you need, or when you go without one? When we go to the grocery store without a list of the things we want, we often forget what we're looking for. We pass by things we need and have to go back for them after we've already been sitting in line to cash out. It's very unorganized and messy. Yet, this is what most people do, and I still do it all the time, but this is also how most of us live our lives in the grand scheme of things. It's a lot easier to go to the store with a list of everything you want, because your mind will know what to look for, therefore lowering the chances of you passing by something you're seeking; you are more efficient, as you don't have to backtrack and go to other aisles you already went through. You don't forget your wants and needs.

Jotting our dreams and aspirations on paper serves as our grocery list in its own way. This list will bring you close to the edges you seek and bring you closer to your heart. With a list, it becomes harder to pass by opportunities that, otherwise, our mind might not be able to see, even if they're just in front of us. With a list, we don't have to backtrack in life and start all over again. It makes the things we want easier to achieve with less mess, and it instills the instructions in our subconscious to seek ways of achieving them.

Do you ever wonder why you notice some things and others don't? Why you notice the kind of car you drive more than others? Why some types of clothes are more appealing to you than others? Why you hang around with certain people more than others? Or why you love a type of person more than somebody else? This is all caused by what our mind is exposed to. What our subconscious mind constantly sees and experiences is what it tells the conscious mind to seek. Often times we do this without even realizing it. This might explain why somebody stays in an unhealthy relationship or a mediocre job – because that is what their subconscious mind experiences and often times is used to.

This is why we must give our subconscious minds better material. Just like what we feed our bodies dictates the health and appearance of them, the thoughts we feed our minds dictate what they tell our minds to look for more of. This is why you must write the things you seek down and look at them daily. Instill in your mind the things you seek and your mind will subconsciously look for ways to attain them as long as you are constantly reminding it what to look for.

If we look back at history, there are certain clues that are left behind and which point to the act of whatever you seek in your mind: you will find it in the physical world. Take, for example, a verse from the King James Bible, Matthew 7:7: "Ask, and it shall be given to you, seek, and ye shall find; knock and it will be opened to you". The Declaration of Independence was written with clear goals of what this country's founders sought, before the War of Independence began, and to this day it serves as the founding goals of the United States of America. Our goals and dreams have to be put on paper so that we can always go back to them.

When I heard my mentors speak about writing your goals down, it never really hit my heart as to the purpose of the action, and so I would do it for a couple of days and then I would forget about it. I would just tell myself, 'well, it's all in my head, I know what I want'. Again, the problem is that the noise of everyday life drowns out these goals and they become blurry in our mind... and we eventually forget them. Before I really embraced writing down my goals and really breaking them apart in detail, it had to make sense to me. As I started writing down my goals and edges as I wanted to feel them in life, I started to notice a couple of reasons why it made absolute perfect sense.

As you sit and think about the things in life which you want to attain, your wants become clearer. In order to truly seek what our hearts want, we are forced to really listen to our hearts. It's very easy to say that your goal is to make a million dollars. That is not your heart speaking, though; that's your ego or some belief instilled in your mind by society. As you set your goals, dig deeper and ask yourself what really makes your heart beat when you think about your wants. When your heart speaks to you, it speaks with the purpose of the universe, and that is to translate love into the physical world. It doesn't say, 'I want to make a millions dollars so I can buy an expensive car and an expensive house'. If your heart were to speak with this end in mind, it would say, 'I want to make a million dollars so I can give my family a better standard of living or be able to spend more time with them'. This is what happens when you sit down and write your goals down. It gives you time to really listen to your heart and block out your ego.

Once you have your goals clearly defined and written, the list will serve as a filter to other shiny objects that might keep you from achieving your dreams. We live in a constantly changing world, with constant development of new opportunities. It's very easy to get away from our goals if they are not clearly defined. A college student's dream might be to study ocean life, as she has always been intrigued by the sea, but then society puts in front of her the shiny object of an office job right out of school that pays far more than a marine biologist would make, and she gravitates towards that shiny object... and her dream is lost forever in time. We can't rely on our willpower to stay true to our desired courses. You need powerful reminders to keep you true to your heart. When you write your heart's desires with meaning behind them, this serves as your beacon in a world full of shiny objects.

I noticed that, once I had my goals clearly written, it became easier to take action. Why? Because it was easier to see the breakdown on paper, rather than try to siphon my goals out of all the thoughts in my mind. I knew that the goals I had written were written down at a time where I was listening to my heart. It's not always possible to listen to our hearts, especially with the fast pace of life today. As I read my goals every day, it's easier to say, "okay, this is what my purpose for today is". See, the moment I write a goal down, for a split second, I feel it in my gut. I feel fear and excitement, and in that moment I can either choose to focus on my fear – which will keep me frozen from taking any action – or I can focus on the actual written goal and begin to take action. Having the goal written down gives me comfort that it's there, and many times evokes images of myself achieving the goal, which motivates me to work even harder to achieve it.

The last thing is that, once you have your list, it will serve as checkpoints along the way to keep you motivated to think bigger. Once you accomplish your first goals you set and have checked them off the list, this gives you confidence that you can achieve what you set your mind to. I believe in this method so much that, even with my small goals for the day, I prewrite them the night before and set the list right on top of my laptop since the first thing I usually do in the morning to begin work is open my laptop. The first thing in the morning that I see is my list, and throughout the day, I cross out the tasks I've finished. The most rewarding part is, at the end of your day, the list serves as your cheerleader. It gives you a pat on the back as you see all your goals crossed out.

I break down my lists in three parts. I have my daily to-do list that I make the night before. I also have my yearly goals with specific times on when I want to achieve them, and I have my long term goals list, which are my lifetime goals which I want to achieve.

In our world today, it can be hard to find encouragement and find others who celebrate your accomplishments. There are too many people in this world who feel less when they see others accomplish their dreams. They become jealous and deep down envious of what you have achieved. I have seen this with coworkers, friends, and even family members. You need to be your own cheerleader, and by writing down your goals and seeing yourself accomplish them, this process will serve as your encouragement to keep walking forward in your journey to get closer to the edges.

School Schedule

After I finished school, I started working a corporate job and my planned schedule seemed to end after I finished work. Once I left work, I had no planned schedule on the things that I needed to do to get closer to my heart, or which edges I wanted to seek. Just like you had a set school schedule for learning, we need to set one for ourselves after work. During this part of our day is where we do things to get closer to our hearts and head towards growth. This is the extra oomph that leaders, artists, entrepreneurs, healers, and professional athletes put in each day to reach their hearts' callings as they seek their edges.

Once you begin to seek your edges and get closer to your heart, this is the time where it's able to be done. Life can become extremely busy, where there is always something to do. It makes it difficult to further promote our growth and further express the universal purpose. We can make ourselves as busy as we want, but what matters is the activities that we focus on. You have to set a school-like schedule after work. It doesn't matter what type of job you have – this can be done. Even setting an hour out of the day for yourself to seek your edges will bring you closer to fulfilling your most important need and to follow your heart.

The biggest problem we all have is finding time to do this. Many of us use the excuse of just being too busy or not having enough time. That's one of the biggest factors that kept me from focusing on the things that I wanted to do and experience. The thing is, if we all look around at the activities that fulfill our days and start to get rid of the unnecessary ones (that are not must do's), we start to find time. One of the main actions I took to find more time and stick to my "school schedule" was limiting the amount of time I spend watching tv shows, news, social media, etc..

The biggest benefit of this was that it opened up more time during my day to focus on my edges. I had more time to give to the people around me, and I had more time to focus on my health and spirituality. I had more time to focus on my heart. It's really hard in the beginning, but after a while, you just get used to it. As far as social media goes, I know many people out there say to completely get rid of it or that it doesn't do anything for you, but I think social media is a way to bring each other closer, even if it's remotely. It's never going to be better than face-to-face interaction, but it's a good way to keep within reach those you have met throughout life. A long lost cousin or old mentor... one may need to reach them one day. Almost as if we are all attached with strings, and any time we want to connect with someone, we have the ability to tug on their string. I gave myself a specific time during the day to check on social media, and after this specified time, I wouldn't check it again.

At night, I write the things I need to do the next day so that when I wake up I don't have to even think: it's all just there and ready to go. I compare this to going to the gym. I used to go to the gym all the time, and without a workout list. I would simply say, "okay, today I'm going to work on shoulders or on cardio," and I would just look for machines that work out my chosen area, or I would think of workouts to complete. My friend Anthony Alayon a bestselling fitness author, recommended that I start taking a workout list to the gym. So, instead of going to the gym and just looking for things to do, I would take a prewritten workout list with me. This made a huge difference in the rate at which I improved my physical health. I was able to work out more, and in a shorter period of time. The list eliminated the period where you are thinking about what to do next. I was able to tailor my workouts more as I was able to break down my workouts in more detail as I created more lists. I created a workout list in my cellphone for each day of the week and broke down each day to a specific goal I wanted to accomplish while I was there. It was easy to have all of this on my phone, so when I got to the gym, all I would do is open up my phone and find a routine to do.

Just by this one simple change, I was able to improve my health and fitness greatly. I was able to develop a great knowledge of workout routines and focus even more on my health. It also made me more efficient at the gym, so it opened up more time for other things. The level of order and focus I was able to obtain by having a list ready before I entered the gym would be impossible to obtain without having a predefined outcome. I thought, "if just by implementing this simple action of adding a to-do list to my gym routine, imagine what could happen if I applied this to my goals list". The importance of sitting down and writing a set schedule for our day, and sticking to our list, becomes one of the most essential factors if we want to head in the direction where our edges lie and where our heart speaks.

The Spark

When you hear your heart's calling, it's hard to decide to start right away. When you hear the calling, is when your mind will start talking to you. Like I mentioned before, our instinctual mind wants to keep us from spending unnecessary energy on the unknown. We automatically start to come up with scenarios, and some of them we can't even fathom... and yet we allow them to affect our actions. Some of those scenes are so far in the distance that they are hard to see and believe in. We are in a current state where we are so disconnected from the vision and possibility that it becomes hard to even believe in ourselves. We try to reason with ourselves as to why we should not follow our visions.

I've always wondered what has made men move forward in times of extreme uncertainty, and make a decision knowing that their vision is very far out there – yet they begin to move forward. For example, there's the story of Alan Turing, who took on a journey that was deemed impossible... yet, he believed with all his heart that he would be able to accomplish it. That was to break the enigma machine code that as a result, played a big role in defeating the Nazis. What is the spark that makes us take on a journey that at first we think is impossible? That spark is the universal courage. The universe rewards those who walk blindly and walk along the dark, unknown path, being guided by the heart. We all have a higher form of ourselves that is waiting to be heard. When we have a certain amount of courage, we begin to walk forward.

Though you feel that calling, some of us will live all our lives and never have enough courage to just follow our hearts, while others react very quickly and in desperation, as they might not have enough time. The decision-maker is always going to depend on how much courage you are going to build up.

The First Couple of Steps

As you being taking your first steps of action in following your heart, you will feel nervous and anxious. Fear talks to you, but you also begin to hear your heart louder and you being to walk on your journey of following what your heart has set you out to do; you then experience a great amount of joy, and love. The world becomes more colorful, it becomes easier to wake up every morning, we are more enthusiastic with the world around us, and the most important thing begins to happen... all of a sudden, it becomes easier to feel and see the love around us. Our heart begins to open to the world around us more, and our creative selves comes out, but all of this can quickly fade in times of hardship, but we must push forward.

I actually realized this one day when I was watching an interview with Elon Musk. He was talking about his success after creating Paypal and that he received a lot of negative feedback from those around him, when spoke about starting a space exploration company. Elon Musk had already acquired a fortune through Paypal and people were asking why he was going to spend millions of dollars on something so risky. He stated that deep down, his calling was to expand human consciousness on what the possibilities of human ingenuity and space exploration. He had already achieved success and riches, yet he was not content. I believe that his heart was calling on him to pursue the edges of human ingenuity, and thus he has shown the world these capabilities, by getting us closer to the edges of solar, electric and space exploration.

There's no amount of money that completely shuts your heart. Money can drown its voice by creating more noise around you, but there will always be that moment where you can't escape your own voice. The moment where everything around you slows and quiets down, and then all of a sudden, your heart speaks to you. The world becomes very real to us in that specific moment and your heart hopes that, by then, you have developed enough courage to believe in it and begin to move forward. This is why you can become the richest and most popular man in the world, and yet there will be those times when you will sit in your room, alone, asking yourself why you didn't truly follow your heart all along, as well as the purpose your heart called you for.

It's a very real thing and it affects all of us. Some of us live in this constant state, and many times we lie to ourselves for so long that we start to believe that the lie is a truth. Always remember it's never too late to follow what we believe our hearts call us for. Whether you currently feel like you have been a bad parent, an unloving spouse, an uncaring friend, that you've treated your body unhealthily, or that you have lost touch with the world or your heart, it's never too late to decide to walk back to your edges and follow your heart. Your heart will guide you with the purpose of love.

Listen Closely

I'm sure you're asking, how do you listen to your heart? Our hearts/higher selves will talk to us in an emotional way. That is why we must listen to ourselves closely. What gives you joy? What makes you feel alive? What were your dreams while growing up? What makes your heart race? What brings about fear?

Imagine your mind as a plant with thousands of roots and rootlets branching out into the ground. The heart is what tells the seed (mind) to start growing. As we grow, every experience we encounter is another root. As the plant lives, the heart whispers... "grow... grow, feel the warmth of the sun as closely as you can, feel the air as much as you can, explore the ground as much as you can and release as much oxygen as you can into the earth", essentially telling/pushing it to feel its outer edges. Our hearts work in the very same way. It constantly speaks to us and tells us to grow by expressing ourselves as we are to the world.

If we stop listening to our hearts and pushing to our edges, we stop growing, and thus in a way, we start dying. We come to the world to experience its beauty and love. I believe it's the way the natural universe had to be. Human consciousness came into existence in order to be the translator of the beauty, love, and magnificence that appears in our world today. Existence on earth is a gift to us from the universe, and I had to see it as such in order to begin to listen to my heart more closely and take action to follow it. Don't be afraid to face your fears and get closer to your edges, as this will build courage to listen to your heart and begin to take action.

Most of the time we struggle with this part of our lives. Many of us just don't know how to listen to our hearts. It's not easy; it can actually be very hard. I believe that we have to develop intense realism in ourselves and in the world around us. We must try to see things as they are and not through the lens of our fears and past circumstances. We must take time to sit quietly and think.... Why did I enjoy doing that so much when I was young? Why was I so passionate about that cause? Why did I first fall in love with that person? These are some of the questions we have to ask ourselves to get to our cores.

Often times, the younger we were in our lives, the more we tended to follow our hearts. When we are young, our fear tends to be weak. It tries to speak to us when we are following our hearts, but we choose to pay very little attention to it. I know because, when I was young, I did a lot of things that, if I were to think about doing them now, fear would have more power and stop me from going forward with them.

For example, when I look back at one of the things I've always been fascinated by is machines, especially airplanes. During my childhood I loved building model airplanes and would often take different model airplane parts and try to customize my own plane out of them. As I grew into my teen years, I remember taking things apart and learning about the inner workings of them and often times trying to figure out how to fix them such as my car or even a blender. I didn't gravitate towards these things because they were labeled by society as cool or because I would obtain something if I did. I simply did them because that's what my heart gravitated towards, but why did this passion fade as I entered college? Maybe because society stepped in and told me that I had to pick a career and something that was suitable for society's view at the young age of eighteen. Once college started it became almost a race where you could only focus on the subjects at hand and also work to pay for college, so very little time was left for me to listen to my heart. Most of the choices I started to make were based on fear and comfort. I became too afraid to open up my heart to the things that really mattered, and also stopped translating the love of my heart to the world around me. I stopped following my universal purpose and became controlled by my fears of the unknown, and could no longer hear my heart at times..

This is a normal part of life. There are those who deviate so much from their hearts that they become lost and no longer hear it. There are those who deviate from their hearts, and yet find their way back. This is the daily fight of the world, where the scales are constantly tipped based on how many of us stay the course of following our hearts, and those who stray away from them. Remember that you can always go back to your heart, regardless of what you have done in the past or what your current state is. We must understand, though, that we have to be aware and take time to listen to it... and to strive for the edges.

Universal Purpose and Our Higher Selves

Our hearts' callings will change throughout our lives. The only static (universal) purpose is to translate the beauty and gift of life during our existences here. The actions that we take to translate these qualities will often times change, during the course of our lives. As our hearts in conjunction with our subconscious dictate the ways we manifest them are based on our current states, they will speak when the opportunity is presented to us. As we grow up, we all question our so called greater purpose... Also when I speak about our purpose in life, I don't mean something that is predestined from the moment we are born, our purpose is created by us as we follow our hearts. We all want to find it. We admire those who do, as when we find it, life tends to unfold in a more beautiful and meaningful way.

I never realized this until I had moved from everything I knew after college to work a corporate job where my creativity and individualism were suppressed. As I lived out of hotel rooms, constantly traveling from place to place, I spent a lot of time by myself. Amidst those lonely times, I was able to hear my heart speak again. These were some of the first questions that my heart asked: "Is this you purpose?" "Is this what you were meant to do?" "Who are you?" I couldn't answer any of these questions. In a way, I had lost myself. I didn't really know who I was or where I was going. In the middle of all that, I was actually getting a masters and applying to medical school, but not really having a true reason why. I was doing it because that's what I had deemed was respectful for society. That's what society's purpose was for me, but I was not listening to my heart. I realized that I had to figure out who I was and what I felt I could do to get closer to who I really was.

During that time, I was very frustrated, and I felt lost, as I had no one really to guide me. What could I do to find myself again and really get in touch with my higher self, and get away from my ego? We all have a very deep yearning to find our purposes. There are times when you feel empty because you don't feel purposeful. I felt guilty many times, that I wasn't doing enough to find mine. There are even times where we just think we have no purpose at all. I felt like this many times. Where I would sit in my office, staring at my email, and every time a new email came in or the phone rang, somehow I wished it was a change or a new opportunity that would get me away from what I was currently doing. I knew deep inside that my heart was calling and I had to answer it. I wanted to answer it, but I had a fear of it. I had the fear that I would start listening to it, yet would never find my purpose, and even be more let down. I don't know if I was more comfortable just not listening to my heart and living with the hope that I would just run into my purpose someday, or go on a journey to find it. I was in a constant push and pull, not knowing what to do.

It's impossible for me to tell you what your exact purpose in life is. Just like we all have uniquely different fingerprints, we all have uniquely different lives. We all have a calling to answer, but what I realized is that you can't beat yourself up over not knowing what it is; the journey of life is just that, creating your purpose. Many of us won't realize what our purpose really is until we have actually taken action and walked on the path that our hearts lead us toward.

There is a commencement speech by Steve Jobs where he says that he never knew how all the dots were going to connect when he was following his passion. He had no idea how things were going to work out when he was starting Apple, yet he took action. He says that it wasn't until he looked back at everything he did that he was able to see how all the dots connected. It's very freeing, looking at our lives in this way. As we strive every day to seek our edges, whether they are our edges of love, action, passion, adventure, happiness, charity, or care for the world, we will eventually be able to connect the dots and unravel our purposes.

Nobody can tell you what your purpose is; only your heart can help you figure that out. What I can tell you is some of the things I started doing to get closer to my own higher self and begin to follow my heart's calling. I started asking myself a series of questions that would serve almost as data points in a chart to help me figure out which path I could take to follow my heart and get closer to my purpose. Just like the Coast Guard searches for the wreckage of a boat, we must search for our own purposes. The Coast Guard will first rely on last communications and coordinates given by the ship in question before an accident occurred. Then they will know a general area of where to look. They will look at the ocean/wind currents to calculate where the boat and survivors might have drifted to. Then they find the debris from the boat, which then are plotted on a map. They start finding more and more debris, which lets them know that they are closer to finding the boat as more points are plotted on the search map. They now have a more defined area of where to look. As they keep searching, they eventually find the survivors and the wreckage of a ship based on all these clues and data points they've found and charted.

I began by finding the things that gave me energy. We live in a world of constant energy exchange. Remember the law of conservation of energy: energy cannot be created nor destroyed, it can only be… transferred. When we do things that are in conjunction with our hearts' callings, we are fulfilled with energy. When we do things that are not in alignment with our hearts, energy is sucked out of us. Write down the things that give you energy, that constantly fulfill you with joy, drive and passion.

One can see the difference in someone who loves to interact with others, yet has a job which involves very little human interaction, or someone who loves to be outside in nature, yet is forced to give that up because his/her spouse dislikes the same. It's very hard to live an energetic life when you are not doing the things that your heart calls you to do. It becomes a constant uphill battle with yourself. Look and write down the things that give you energy, and follow the edges of that. Does doing yoga fill you with energy? Keep pursuing that to the edges which you can reach. Maybe you will become an instructor or maybe you will meet someone there that will serve as an inspiration to seek another part of your purpose. When I tell people this, some of them say, "Well, what if I'm wasting my time seeking something that might be trivial, like pursuing a hobby?" My argument to that is, if it's something that gives you energy, or gives you joy in pursuing it, then consider that as a dot of a part of your journey. Only when you have connected all the dots will your purpose reveal itself, but in the meantime, we must constantly seek to add more dots to our charts by repeatedly doing the things that fulfill us with positive energy, and only then will we get closer to knowing our purposes. This is how we connect and find our higher selves; yes, the Coast Guard could have simply taken no action in searching for the boat, and believed in their minds that it was going to be impossible to find the boat due to the large size of area they had to cover and the unknown journey they had to take... but they wouldn't. Look for the little things that fill you with energy, and continue to pursue them.

Tim Ferris says, " The question you should be asking isn't, "what do I want? Or "what are my goals?" but "what would excite me?" As we live in a world in which we are normally judged by the size of our bank account, it's very easy to ask ourselves the wrong questions. Usually, when you ask people what their goals are, the goal of having more money is stated as one, it having the biggest importance. The problem with this mentality is that someone can achieve the goal, and yet still feel that emptiness in their heart. This happens because we ask ourselves the wrong questions.

This is what happened to many of us today. We asked ourselves what our wants were as we entered the real world of adulthood and became blinded by the infiltration of society's purpose on our minds. Our egos were created, and thus our egos called for us to make more money and fit in with society. Instead, we should have been asking ourselves, what are the things that bring in excitement to our lives? If you live your life by asking yourself this question, it will keep you in line with your heart, regardless of the monetary awards that are promised by your ego and society.

Ask yourself about the past experiences in your life that have made you feel very alive. Did you feel alive when you played your first song on your guitar? Did you feel alive when you volunteered in the soup kitchen? Did you feel alive when you made that recipe? Did you feel alive when you helped someone get through a bad situation? Did you feel alive when you embraced someone you love?

These are the clues and data points we eventually collect. They are the breadcrumbs left behind by our purpose, for us to be able to trace over and find it. Don't be afraid to follow the things that make you feel alive, regardless of what society or other people think is right. You love to paint? Paint! You love to sing? Sing! You love to cook? Cook! You love to code? Code! Do you love to be out in nature? Go out there! Your dream, growing up, was to fly planes? Learn to fly!

There are so many small clues in our daily lives that, if we only chose to follow them, would open up endless possibilities for our growth and abilities to project our love to the world in countless ways. Before we can become more efficient at translating the gift of life to the outer world, we must first understand ourselves better. Many of us don't take the time out of our day to better understand ourselves. Many times, our wants and the things we tend to pursue are driven by the world around us. We make decisions based on whether we think society (parents, friends, etc.) will like the results. Yet, most of the time, we don't even ask ourselves if doing that very thing will excite us.

For example, when I finally got into medical school, I realized I didn't want to do it anymore. I didn't feel it in my heart: I had worked so hard to get in, retaking MCAT tests, pursuing a master's degree to improve my chances at getting in, and yet when I got the letter of acceptance, I wasn't sure. I think, perhaps, that this is because it was the first time in a while where I had actually questioned myself as to what made me excited. The medical field is a wonderful field of study, full of opportunities, and is one in which you can greatly translate your love for the world as you care for the ill. I just thought about the fact that I'd chosen to be a doctor because it was one of the professions I had chosen to be when I'd first started college. Why did I choose that at eighteen years old? I had no idea what a doctor did, other than to help the sick and make a good living. I think I chose that because it sounded like an important job that paid well and was involved in helping others, and there was also the fact that I had to choose my major at the start of college. I realized, at twenty-four years old, that I didn't know myself well enough to put a bet on something that I'd chosen when entering college.

"What ever happened to all the things I learned in college?" I would ask myself. The lessons that I learned from all the people I met. All those experiences of love and growth. Did those just not mean anything? Did they not change me as a person? Of course they did. My way of thinking was a bit different than it had been at the age of eighteen. Maybe I just hadn't found my purpose yet. Maybe that experience was necessary for me to be able to get closer to unraveling my purpose, and maybe one day I would. I do know, though, that our hearts' callings will change according to the experiences we've lived through and our views of the world. I heard my heart at that moment, telling me to continue walking, and I chose to follow it and walk past the turn to the path that would have led me to become a doctor.

The worst thing one can do is to never take the time to ask one's self the right questions. Remember that it is never too late to make a decision to change whatever you've been doing and begin to follow your heart. This is what will sustain you through life. Think about the things that you constantly think about when you are by yourself. What do you normally tend to gravitate towards in your free time? What passions can you blend together to do something meaningful for the world to see? What kind of things do you feel passionate about when talking to other people? And most important of all, what would you do if money was not an object? These were some of the questions I started to ask myself after I decided not to go to medical school. I have met extremely joyful and energetic wealthy people, but have also met unkind and egotistic rich people. If we want to stay on the right direction of following the universal purpose, we must not choose our paths based on the purpose of acquiring more money. There has to be a greater meaning behind what you seek, and it starts with your heart. As your heart calls on you to seek different edges of your life, you must always remain true to it and ask the right questions that bring you closer to your purpose.

Know Yourself and Take Action

The moment you understand and realize what your current passion is (as long as it is positive and productive), you must take whatever measures are needed to start seeking it. Have you always wanted to volunteer overseas to help others? Is your heart calling you to become a better parent? To follow your dream of starting your own business? To do something positive for the world? You must start today. Start with what you know and look for the opportunities around you which you can actively pursue to get closer to your edge – of whatever your heart calls you for. Seek your strengths and use those to serve as guides of the paths you should seek and weaknesses in which you must strengthen. After you get in the habit of actively seeking the opportunities to get closer to your edge, you will start becoming more aware of yourself and the present world around you.

Find the current opportunities you can seek today, so that you can continue to walk towards the edges which your heart calls you towards. When you combine all these different journeys, your purpose will then start unraveling itself. As you seek your edges and look for ways to get you closer to what your heart calls you for, you will become optimistic and develop more faith in your heart. Whether you are cleaning hotel rooms and aspiring to be able to help your kid pay for college, or running a fortune 500 company and looking to get in touch with your family again, you essentially have equal choices on working towards following your heart's calling. We all face these same choices every day, and ultimately have the power to take action.

Nobody can force you to follow your heart; only you can make that choice. This is really freeing, as all of our situations around us become less significant in relation to the kind of lives we live. Many of us become victims to the world around us, and our current situations also become our excuses to not seek to feel our edges. Some of us will blame our significant other for the inability to follow our hearts, but don't understand that the power to make that choice belongs all along to us. I love the quote by Viktor Frankl – *"Everything can be taken from a man but one thing: The last of human freedoms – to choose one's attitude in any given set of circumstances, to choose one's own way"*. This quote is so powerful because Viktor Frankl was a holocaust survivor who endured such a terrible part of his life as he witnessed the horrors and evil acts during the Holocaust. Everything was taken from him, except one thing, and that is to choose if he was going to let the Nazis take his basic human freedom away from him, the right to choose his way.

At any moment, we all have the right to choose to follow our hearts' callings, as there is always a way to follow our hearts. Sometimes even the smallest opportunities lie in front of the most difficult situations, and we simply have to be aware and look for them at all times. We essentially need to wake up and realize that it is up to us, and we sometimes must start with the smallest opportunities that lie in front of us, but we must take action.

A Science Experiment on Yourself

Most people think of chemistry as reactions of molecules or elements. I believe that chemistry and physics can be applied to our daily lives. I mean, everything in the universe is made up of atoms, which make up molecules, and molecules make up elements, which are the basic building blocks of life. About 99% of the mass of our bodies is made up through an interaction between different elements that consist of oxygen, carbon, hydrogen, nitrogen, calcium, and phosphorous. Most of us don't think of our bodies in this way. We essentially forget that we are all children of stars. It sounds geeky or deep, but essentially, that's what we are, regardless of whether you believe in creation or evolution. The elements that exist in the universe were combined to create our bodies and minds. These are real world principles that set the conditions for our everyday lives.

It's very difficult to look at life this way, but I want to give you a different perspective to allow you to think about it, and maybe you will look at things a bit differently, or maybe it might even make more sense to you in relation to what I'm about to explain. Action is something I've thought a lot about. Why do some people take massive action on their hearts' callings, yet some of us would rather sleep in and stay in our warm beds? This was me before I changed, and even to this day, I still feel some resistance when getting out of bed, but this resistance tends to become weaker the more I triumph over it.

I have a science background, and chemistry lab was actually one of the classes I enjoyed a great deal. Reactions always amazed me... how, by mixing two different compounds, I would create something completely different from what the other two compounds had been. The process of taking action to follow our hearts and get closer to our edges is essentially a chemical reaction in progress. 'Activation energy' is a term coined by a Swedish scientist, Svante Arrhenius. Arrhenius theorized that, in order for a chemical system with different reactants to react, they needed a certain amount of activation energy in order for the reaction to move forward or begin. Thus, activation energy is the minimum energy that is required to start the action of interaction between elements. Not to go too deep into this, but most elements have different rates of reactions. Some elements like to react with other elements more than others, and some like to be in a stable state and don't like to change. Therefore, a certain amount of activation energy is needed to change the state of one in order for it to begin to react, almost as if one was forcing or exciting it into starting the reaction. This energy comes in many different forms, such as heat, electrical, physical, or chemical.

This same thing happens to us on a daily basis. There are many ideas that our hearts speak out to us with, as needs in order to fulfill our heart's calling. Just like we need to feed our bodies, we also have to feed our hungry hearts. When it speaks to you in hunger, you must strive to feed it the best of what it asks for. For example, as I write this book, there are times when I turn my computer on and struggle to start writing. My heart calls on me to write and seek the edges of contribution to the world, but there are so many other things I can be doing that are easier, such as checking my mail, going on social media, reading the news, or watching television. Before I get in my car to go the gym, there's a certain amount of willpower I have to produce to overcome the resistance of not going. Before I decide to try something new, there's a certain amount of mental and physical energy I need to input to overcome the resistance. I'm essentially a molecule that interacts with the world, and there's a certain amount of energy I need to input to begin my re-ACTION towards what my heart calls on me for, and to create art for the physical world to see.

What do I do to combat the resistance of not writing? I have to invest a certain amount of energy to combat this inert state of not doing what I'm supposed to be doing. I have to input energy to force myself to start investing time into the book. The barrier that I need to break through is that I know that starting to work on the book is going to require a lot of deep thinking and focus, while my mind is telling me all the other fun things that I could be doing instead. Fear has talked to me and has told me that I'm not a writer. Yet, I have to input enough energy to start getting me to write. That moment and energy input to propel me to start taking action is the activation energy required to overcome my fear and discomfort. If one could measure it, it would be a measure of energy... whether it's a mix of mental and/or physical energy. This has been very freeing, to look at motivation in this manner. Our wants and actions are essentially elements waiting to react in order to create whatever your heart has been calling you to do. Every battle between your heart and your mind/fear requires a certain amount of activation energy to surpass the block that is keeping you inert and from seeking your heart's calling.

Remember that, for every want and action, you will feel a bit different. Some will require less energy input and, for others, you will need substantial amounts of it, depending on the want and required action, but each one requires energy input from you. Another factor that can be used to speed up a reaction is a catalyst. A catalyst is a substance that lowers the activation energy required to get a reaction started. A catalyst that we can use for ourselves to lower the amount of energy we must input to begin taking action for what we believe our hearts call us for is meaning. A catalyst can be someone you love, or a deep powerful outcome you want to produce as a result of taking action. I compare a catalyst to our drive. What drives you to paint? Is it because you want the world to see your art, or are you doing it to better the quality of your life through being able to sell it and make a living? When we have a catalyst, we tend to take more action and feel less resistance. The more of a drive we have to follow our hearts, the faster we take action towards achieving our hearts' needs.

In essence, striving to feel the edges of life is not easy. You will always feel some measure of resistance as you begin to take action to follow your heart and feel the outer edges. Some of them will feel impossible at first, but remember that everything has a certain amount of activation energy. The things that mean the most to us, are the ones that require the most energy, but it is up to us to input this energy by repeatedly taking action despite the resistance we feel. Every single chemical reaction in the universe can be activated, just as long as enough energy is put into it to get it started. It all boils down to how much energy you are willing to put into it and how much discomfort you are willing to feel to get to your desired outcome.

Part Five- Growth: Our Most Basic Need

"Ever since I was a child I have had this instinctive urge for expansion and growth. To me, the function and duty of a quality human being is the sincere and honest development of one's potential." –Bruce Lee

We all have our own fears, doubts, and insecurities. They might be projected in different ways, but they are there. Many times, we feel as if we're different because we feel fear when it comes to striving to feel the edges of our lives. We can be pretty harsh on ourselves at times, because we think that we shouldn't feel fear or have doubts about how things are going to turn out. I used to think everyone else had it figured out except me. Why did so many of my friends know in college what they wanted to be? Why was I the only person that hadn't found their purpose? Why was I the only person that felt I wasn't reaching my full potential? The problem with this kind of thinking is that we all have these feelings. Even the most popular kid in school feels alone and unworthy at times. The famous model can feel insecure about her body. Thomas Edison doubted himself. Even the bravest soldier on the battlefield can feel fear.

You are not alone. It is perfectly normal to feel like this at times, but the most important part about these feelings is that you must conquer them in order to be able to grow. Self-growth is one of the most important and basic human needs. Abraham Maslow was a psychologist who studied human behavior and came up with the basic order of human needs. He set up the needs in a pyramid chart, where the most fundamental basic need is at the bottom of the pyramid, and as each need is fulfilled, the next basic need is above it. Maslow's hierarchy of needs starts with physiological needs, then safety, then love and belonging, then self-esteem, and lastly, self-actualization or growth.

We live in a time where, fortunately, many people have the first two basic needs met, but for some reason remain stuck on love and belonging. Many of us work jobs just to be able to afford nicer things or be a normal participant in society in order to feel like we belong and feel loved. For many of us, we stop at this level and fight for all of our lives to acquire the basic need of love and belonging, so that we forget the other two, self-esteem and growth. Many of us live our lives being discontent, with the feeling that something is missing. The feelings of fear, hurt, doubt, and insecurity are the signals your body gives you when those two needs are not being met. When your body needs food, you feel hungry. When your body needs water, you feel thirsty. When your heart is being kept in the dark, life tends to become more monotonous and meaningless. That's the signal your mind gives you when you are not living your life by seeking your edges. In order to get closer to the edges of life, we must constantly grow in all aspects of our lives.

Growing, essentially gets us closer to our higher selves and gives us a better understanding of the world around us. From the moment we are born, we begin to grow rapidly, both physically and mentally. We start to see and understand the world around us just enough to get us by. We are constantly pushed to new experiences and learning by society. We go to school and learn about different subjects of the world, such as science, math, and history. We also learn a bit about ourselves and the different edges of our lives. Our growth is interdependent on the current place we live, and we might be more limited in growth than others, but we still grow in different aspect of our lives. As we enter adulthood, we often times become confused as to what we are supposed to do. All of our lives, we have been pushed to grow, either forcibly by school, parents, or overall society, so that when some of those drivers are all of a sudden taken away from us, we become dependent on ourselves as the drivers to grow.

Our parents and school are no longer in the picture, and we are solely left by society to drive us most of the time. We go with the societal norms, get jobs, make as much money as we can, buy stuff, get married, have kids, and retire. All these factors now become the drivers of our lives. Instead of parenting ourselves, we leave society to do the parenting for us. This can create a large block in our hearts, where it becomes hard to listen and follow. We tell ourselves it is too late... "I'm too old, I'm being foolish by following my heart, and I just don't have the time". Literally, society gets in the way of our hearts and blinds us from where the edges of our lives lie.

The pressures of society to pay our mortgages, have high-paying jobs, climb the corporate ladders, and keep up with the joneses has made it very difficult to seek the things we truly want, and to grow as we seek our edges. Many of just don't know any better, as this is what we've seen all throughout our lives. This is what we watch on television, this is what we experience as we grow up, and eventually we are exposed to it so much that we believe this is what everybody does.

It's like the ludicrous and inhumane process of training an elephant. A baby elephant will get one leg chained up during training. In the beginning, he pulls and fights it with all his might, but he's yet to be strong enough to brake the chain. The baby elephant becomes extremely frustrated and pulls on the chain continuously until he is broken down over time. He has been conditioned to know that the chain is incredibly strong and he cannot break it, that once he becomes an adult and has enough strength to brake the chain, the opposite actually happens. He doesn't try tugging on the chain any longer, because he has been conditioned to know that pulling on the chain is useless.. He has been trained by it so much that he simply just does not know any different. This is why I say it's not easy to just begin to follow our hearts and do the things that we believe are important.

We are so conditioned by society that following our hearts is risky, and that after a while, we no longer listen to it, and become driven by what society wants of us. This is why it becomes hard to listen to our hearts. We can't hear it anymore because we no longer hear it amidst all the noise. It's like when I used to wait tables in college. There were always the same songs that played in the restaurant, and after a while, I would get so caught up into work that I no longer really heard the music. It's hard to explain, but it's as if we simply become numb to it. Just like that, our hearts are only felt and heard in rare moments. Society has overshadowed our wants and has kept us at bay from doing anything out of the ordinary.

Autopilot Engaged

Have you ever seen the movie *Click*? It's a movie about a family man who finds a remote control that can pause or fast-forward his life at any moment he chooses. So, what does he do? He begins to fast-forward certain aspects of his life, such as fast-forwarding his current life through until his next work promotion. His next door neighbor keeps buying new things and he is tired of seeing them show off all these toys, so he decides to fast-forward to the next promotion still, and he fast-forwards his life so much to reach these certain accolades of his work life, so that he wakes up rich, alone, and unhealthy. He goes back to the guy that gave him the remote and he asks why this has happened. The man says that, during the fast-forwarding phases, he was on autopilot, just responding to his life with just enough words and emotion to get him by. This is how many of us live our lives. We are so caught up in what society pushes us to do that we essentially live our lives on autopilot until we reach major aspects of our lives, such as graduation from college, our wedding days, the birth of a child, or our next promotion.

No wonder millions of people are dissatisfied with their lives. Life on autopilot is very inanimate and boring. The main goal of your autopilot setting is to get you through the day with as little emotional change as it can. It gets you to interact with others just on a basic level, and it keeps you from expressing your heart to the world. Autopilot keeps you from experiencing the gift of life. It keeps us from living in the present moments. We end up missing so many of the small things in life that actually matter. I hear people, all the time, complaining about how monotonous or boring their life has become, but they do nothing to change their courses. They remain on autopilot most of their lives and, when they do decide to change course and turn off the autopilot, fear kicks in the alarm and tries to get them back into autopilot mode.

As time progresses, we get so used to this that it becomes our norm, and anything else aside from this is fearful. As I stated before, our minds wants to keep us safe and away from experiencing hurt, thus preferring to keep us on autopilot so we don't deviate from this course of safety. The problem with this safety mechanism is that it stuns our general growth. We are all born with similar mental capabilities, unless of course there is a disability or illness that affects these capabilities. Our minds are designed for learning and application. If we all remain in this autopilot state, new ideas, innovation, and appreciation for life are unable to enter our minds. Most of us are simply unaware that we are on autopilot, as autopilot has become our norm. Especially the older we get, the more autopilot becomes our default setting. If you look closely at the world around you, many of the people in your world have been in this autopilot setting. We are all funneled to this certain path of: go to school, get a job, get married in your twenties, have children right after marriage, get the next promotion, and make more money to buy a nicer house/car. If we don't follow on this path, we are seen as odd or we feel bad about ourselves.

Society bullies us into conforming to the norm. Once many of my friends had children, it became difficult to hang out with them and, we stopped doing the things that we loved doing. Even though I realized this was happening, I started to feel the pressure, too. I felt the pressure of having to make more money as I got older, to get married and to get that next promotion. I too started to switch my autopilot on more often as I worked to get to that very thing that society wanted me to achieve. I could see myself walking away from my heart as I tried to please society's wants for me. I was living my life more for the sake of pleasing society than my growth.

This is why the world is the way it is. We have allowed ourselves to become slaves to society's expectations of us. This is why hunger, poverty, and pollution exist, and why people have become more distant from each other. Just like Michael Newman in *Click*, who missed so many aspects of his life while trying to achieve the very thing society wanted him to be, we tend to blind ourselves from seeing the world for what it really is. We become so focused on achieving society's expectations of us that we have been numbed to feeling for a starving child or seeing how the rainforests of the world rapidly disappear from the earth. We can't feel or see these things because most of the world is essentially on autopilot. Our capacity for mental growth has been dwindled down by the very fact that we are being driven by society and not our hearts. We have stopped seeking our true edges in order to please society and to avoid the feeling of fear.

Now, how can you work to disengage your own autopilot? You can accomplish this by constantly growing, facing your fears, and feeling your heart. When you are doing this, you are striving to feel the edges of your life a little closer. We have to seek to grow every day, visit the places of fear in our minds, and constantly open our hearts to the world, regardless of what society thinks of us. The push to grow in all aspects of our lives is a way to shut our autopilot settings off.

Seek to grow deeper relationships with the people around you. Seek to grow your understanding of nature and the impact we have on it. Seek to grow your understanding of where your food comes from and the impact it has on your body. Seek your understanding of the world by constantly learning new things every day and questioning your past beliefs. Seek to grow your understanding of yourself. Seek to grow your potential and the positive impact you have on the world. Seek to grow the openness of your heart and your compassion for others. Seek to always grow towards your true potential and your universal purpose in life.

As you are moving away from the static mode of autopilot, you will feel fear and even rejection. This is just your mind and society's intimidation working to put you back in line, just like everyone else. For the mind, growth can indicate new unknown feelings and places. For society, growth is seen as a change to the status quo. You must seek to be that change by constantly seeking to grow yourself in all aspects of your life, regardless of what society and your mind try to tell you. Always use the edges of your life and your heart as guides to keep you from being on autopilot.

Miracle Child

Growing and seeking to change ourselves seems like a lot of work, right? Seems like a constant battle between ourselves and the world around us, and you might be asking, why should I strive to find my purpose? Why should I seek the edges of my life when I'm perfectly fine with the way my life is right now? I would say that, if you're reading this book right now and you've made it this far, there's something inside of you that's calling you to find that part of the real you which is asking to be discovered. I believe that, at one point or another, we all feel this call. Many of us simply ignore it and go on with our lives, and some of us strive to find it. It's very challenging to look at the big picture of life. Nobody truly knows how we got here and what our role in the universe really is. There is one thing I do know about life, though: that no matter how you put it, life is the most precious gift we can ever receive.

The very gift that was given to us... to be born into this world and experience it for ourselves. Have you ever thought of that? I believe most of us take this gift for granted. The very being of our existence in the world. I think we don't tend to think about it, as life is so busy that most people don't acknowledge their actual existence. I mean, it's hard to fathom what life would be like if you didn't exist. I believe thinking about this gives our life deeper meaning.

I heard a talk by a great author, Mel Robbins, where she explains that scientists have calculated that the chances of someone being born into existence today are one in four hundred trillion. I mean, can you imagine that? Just to give you an idea of how minute that chance is, there are about five hundred billion grains of sand in a standard volleyball court. Now imagine eight hundred volleyball courts lined up together, and a red grain being thrown from an airplane into this space. The chance of finding that red grain of sand in these eight hundred volleyball courts is the chance of you being born today. Look back at a short history of your family tree. Your great grandfather would have had to meet your great grandmother in a sea of many other thousands of women he saw or talked to in the span of his life. Then the right circumstances had to happen in order for them to meet, and then out of millions of sperms, a single one had to find the egg released out of millions of others for your grandmother to be born, and this process of chance can be traced back to your early caveman ancestors. Every single one of these reproductive cycles had to happen in a very specific way in order for you to be born. Just this single cycle of reproduction makes your chances extremely slim, and yet is only one small factor when looking at the grand scheme of things. Such as the chance of survival of each and every single one of them in order to produce the next generation, not to mention the hardships they had to overcome.

You're probably asking, why I am telling you this? I want you to see the miracle that we all are. It's something that people rarely think of, and yet it puts our purpose in perspective. Looking at your life in this way opens up the importance of living your life on the edges. It opens you up to seeking to live your life by seeking and following your heart. It makes our time here incredibly meaningful, and the societal layers that enclose our self, begin to fall off.

In order to honor our time here, and the gift we have been given, we must seek positive growth in all areas of our lives. Everyone born into this world is a miracle child, filled with all the universal love and the right to follow their own chosen paths. We cannot let the small intricacies of life get in the way of our growth. We must never settle for what we believe the societal norm is. And remember, no matter what your past or current situation is, your life is a miracle and you should always treat it as so. Every single one of us living on earth today, regardless of whether you are homeless or the King of England, has been given the same gift. The gift of life.

Sometimes I wonder what life would be if it had never been given the chance to exist on earth today. Where would my loved ones be today if I had never been given the chance to love them? Where would those strangers be if I had never been allowed to help them? Where would my friends be if I had never been given the chance to laugh with them? Where would my brother be if I had never been allowed to embrace him? When I ask myself these questions, I feel great joy and feel extreme gratitude to have received this opportunity to exist. Yet, it's so easy to forget and take for granted the opportunity we have been given. Our souls are allowed to express themselves in the physical realm for a limited amount of time, and will never be allowed to have this opportunity again as far as we know. This is our time to shine and express our hearts to the world around us.

Miracle Grow

You and I are a miracle, and knowing this fact, we should take this opportunity to grow and feel the richness of life. Many of us are deceived into thinking we are experiencing growth when judging how much money we make and the status we hold in society's pyramid. I used to think about growth in a very naïve sort of way. Growth, to me, was having more financial wealth and status. This is how many of us are funneled by society to "grow" and produce. We can compare this to the current way in which meat production is done today. There is a certain industry standard to take an animal, place in a very small tight space, so it's only two choices are to eat and drink water, anything aside from that is seen as going against the industry norm. Thus, if a farmer decides to let his animals roam in pasture and feed from the pasture themselves, they are seen as bad business owners, hippies or tree huggers, when essentially they are doing right, yet are not taken seriously by the economic society, because they are different from the socioeconomic norm. These farmers are seen as odd, because they are putting the lives of their animals and crops in front of profits. Many times, I looked down upon myself if I wasn't making a certain amount of money or living in a certain way. Growth in this manner is very limited, and leaves you feeling empty.

We end up missing out on so many parts of our lives in which we can grow, yet leave these options on the back burner. The process fools us into thinking we are growing, yet we remain underground without being able to see the light. We are taught so many things by school and society, but the book on how to truly grow is left closed. The focus that is put by society for us to learn is on achievement and production. This thinking causes us to live our lives in a constant race to outdo each other, based on what rank we are at in society, yet the most important aspects of growth receive little value.

We essentially become people stranded in the middle of an ocean, trying to climb on top of each other just to keep from drowning. It makes it incredibly hard to really grow when we are left with a very limited set of instructions directing us how to grow and repay the gift of existence. As many of us start reaching adulthood, we experience less intentional growth.. The concept of growth becomes very arduous to continue as we get older because it's hard to listen to our hearts and in some occasions we lie to ourselves that we are, as the pressure of society continues to press upon us. Many of us just give up and live a life with very little real growth.

I had to change my thinking on the way I viewed growth. When I was on a stage in my life, where I felt that I no longer seemed to be proactively seeking real growth, I realized I needed to change the way I was approaching my life. My heart was calling me to seek growth, but I didn't know where to start. My view on personal growth was so distorted that I didn't know where to refocus my energy. It wasn't until I realized that all I had to do was look around me that it happened. I needed to look at all the aspects of my life that were happening, yet I had not been paying them any attention. Growth is more than just learning and achieving more. Growth is about paying attention to the small details of our lives and focusing on how we can use our hearts to get closer to these details.

How close could I get to my mother and father? How much could I feel someone I loved? How much could I help a friend in need? How much of the world could I experience? How much could I learn about myself in order to be able to love others more? How much of my potential could I reach in order to help others reach theirs? How healthy could I get, in order to be able to give off positive energy to others? How much knowledge could I learn in order to give my children better guidance so that they could walk the world better equipped? How much could I grow the belief I had in my dreams? How much could I grow the passion I had in my heart?

The Edges of growth lie all around us. We must not limit our growth to the basic means that society instills in us, such as the push for fitting in and status in the societal hierarchy. Open your heart and look around your life at the ways in which you can start pursuing your real growth as I realized I had to do couple years ago. During that time I was in a constant battle between my societal driven ego and my heart. I had done everything society wanted me to do. I went to college, got a master's, and was able to get a great job and as I entered the "real world", I was, in essence, entering a new stage of my life.

Our lives tend to unfold in specific stages. The biggest events of our lives have a tendency to transpire during the transition between these stages. They serve as signs in the roads of our life, showing that our exits from our existing paths are approaching and we are about to reach our destination. Just like the start of falling leaves indicates the beginning of fall, our lives have these same natural cycles. Once those events happen, we enter our new paths. When we are young, we are constantly traveling and exiting different paths of our lives. As we get older, the exit signs are less frequently seen. We do a lot of driving, as if we're driving on one long highway to a certain destination. The older we get, the longer these highways become, but why?

During our child and teenage years, and even during adulthood, the stages or the destination are often times pre-set for us. The course and way to get there is also programmed so that we have a general idea where we are headed for the most part. These destinations are landmarks like graduating from school, getting a good paying job, buying a home, getting married, having children, and retiring. This is the glue to the human condition. We all drive in these common paths as we strive to reach these destinations. For many of us this is the normal course of life, and we tend to do a lot of growing during these stages. What happens to all the time in between the stages, though? These are the long roads I'm talking about. As we travel to these predefined destinations, why can't we veer of the highway and travel to these destinations using the side roads and exploring other roads as we get there. It's very easy to try and follow a path that already has been traveled. Why can't we explore other areas of our lives, instead of just focusing on these societal driven stages? When we are young we are traveling to these stages, but are exploring other exits that are not marked as we head in our direction toward our specifically marked destination, like for example graduating high school. We seek to find different paths to reach these destinations and, as a result, grow our perspectives and knowledge. We end up taking more exits which lead to different destinations, and end up growing in aspects which our hearts have guided us to.

During the path to graduating from high school, you might learn about true love for another person, you might learn what a broken heart can feel like, you might find a person that will help you listen to your heart closer or will simply introduce you to the love for a sport. We are constantly seeking those things that our heart calls us for during the journey. We take risks for love, we take risks for new experiences, and the amount of learning that we do is immense. This growth is magnified because of the edges or the paths that we explore as we journey on to graduation. I mean, imagine if the only thing you learned in high school were the subjects taught in order to achieve graduation. We would be very robotic creatures. Life would essentially lose its color and we would be significantly unprepared to handle the next stages that follow.

As we enter the real world and grow older, often times, veering off the main course to these predefined stages set by society is seen as strange or we become the oddball of society. Often times it becomes scary to veer off the main path, since society's pressure or learned fear makes us question that if we veer off the path we are going to let society down. Though Robert Frost lets us know that it is ok to stray from the path that has been well traveled in his poem- *The Road Not Taken* in which at the end of the poem he says- "Two roads diverged in a wood, and I- I took the one less traveled by and that has made all the difference".

I remember my friend TJ at the age of twenty eight decided that he was going to quit his job and travel the world. He was responsible about it, worked and saved for over a year and started his journey. He first told me that his family and his coworkers thought he was crazy for doing this and even I heard comments from other friends saying that he was being irresponsible, even I after a while thought he was a little insane for doing something like this. After about a year in his travels I talked to TJ while he was in Australia and from that conversation I understood what his intent was and why some people thought he was odd for doing this. Deep down I believe TJ was following his heart and unlike many of us, actually had the courage to follow it. TJ in a way was veering off the highway that led to these societal destinations and I feel made some people angry with themselves, because maybe they realized they hadn't truly followed their heart after all. In a way TJ became a beacon to the rest of us, as one that was following his heart.

We stop exploring and are afraid to get off the main highway. All of a sudden, we find ourselves in a pack, traveling together to similar destinations. The unknown exits where your heart calls upon you to get off are more frequently ignored. As a result of this, our growth is no longer magnified; it actually becomes very limited in the knowledge and experiences of the universe. We only acquire what we learn as we travel the main highway. The fear to pursue any of these unknown exits seems to get magnified as we get older, which in turn diminishes our growth.

As stated by Albert Schweitzer, *"I don't know what your destiny will be, but one thing I know: the only ones among you who will be really happy are those who will have sought and found how to serve".* The more we tend to seek the Edge of growth in the areas which our hearts calls us for, the closer we get to finding the way in which we can use our existences to serve the world in a positive way. In order to find this path, we must be willing to expose ourselves to the new, and grow.

To Believe What We Can't Feel

Before I began writing this book, I broke down the edges which I felt were the most important, or which represented a large core of our lives. My purpose of talking about these specific edges is that, by understanding them and seeking them in our own lives, may lead us closer to our hearts. I thought a great deal about the Edge of growth. I mean, who am I to tell you how to live your life? Why should you grow? Why is your rate of growth wrong? What if you're perfectly fine not growing to your potential? What if the glass being a quarter full is all the water you need right now?

In some personal development books, I feel that one is just made to assume that the writer has the authority and knowledge to tell you how you should live your life because they are wealthy or popular enough to tell you so. It's just never mentioned that what they are talking about is their experience or their belief. Sometimes I felt bad reading these specific books because I started to feel like I had lived my life in a way that had been wrong all along. So I wanted to give you a core reason that you can think about, and apply it to your reasoning for growth. In simple terms, growth is acquired once one faces their fears and follows their heart. When one begins to walk in the fear of the unknown to reach their heart's calling, during that period, he or she is growing. We learn more about ourselves and our world, meet new people, feel new emotions, and grow the belief in ourselves.

So, why should we strive to grow? What makes this the right way to live? I can't give you that actual reason, because this is a question that has been asked for thousands of years and many philosophers have come up with their own theories in order to try to understand why we are here and what is the right way to live our purposes on earth, but this is what I've realized in my life...

The famous philosopher, Albert Schweitzer, breaks down what our essential laws of thought really are. He explains it beautifully, the relationship between our purpose and our reason for growth. What do we believe is actually true in our lives, or in essence, what is the purpose of our lives in the universe?

Doctor Schweitzer says: *"To analyze Reason fully would be to analyze the will-to-live. The philosophy that abandons the old Rationalism must begin by meditating on itself. Thus, if we ask, "What is the immediate fact of my consciousness? What do I self-consciously know of myself, making abstractions of all else, from childhood to old age? To what do I always return?" we find the simple fact of consciousness is this, I will to live. Through every stage of life, this is the one thing I know about myself. I do not say, "I am life"; for life continues to be a mystery too great to understand. I only know that I cling to it. I fear its cessation – death. I dread its diminution – pain. I seek its enlargement – joy."*

"What shall be my attitude toward this other life? It can only be of a peace with my attitude towards my own life. If I am a thinking being, I must regard other life than my own with equal reverence. For I shall know that it longs for fullness and development as deeply as I do myself. Therefore, I see that evil is what annihilates, hampers, or hinders life. And this holds good whether I regard it physically or spiritually. Goodness, by the same token, is the saving or helping of life, the enabling of whatever life I can, to attain its highest development. This is the

absolute and reasonable ethic. Whether such-and-such a man arrives at this principle, I may not know. But I know that it is given inherently in the will-to-live."

The continual search for growth is instilled in our hearts from the very moments at which we are born. The one thing we can surely know about ourselves if we look inside our hearts, or even examine our instinctual behavior, is that we are all born with the will to live. With this will to live comes the appreciation for life here today, with the purpose to help and protect it. I believe this is the main principle that drives our behavior, and when forgotten, it puts us against life's purpose. This is why there are those who diminish life, as they have lost sight of this universal purpose, but deep inside them, their heart calls on them, and yet they cannot hear it, as its voice is lost in the loudness of the chaos in their mind.

If we look at the big picture, we were born into this world to live here for a certain period of time. Regardless of what religious or scientific belief you have about life itself, what happens after your death? The one factual thing we know is that we are no longer present on earth after we die. We are given the gift to exist in a wonderful place and experience its life. The problem about this fact is that it's very hard to accept our own mortality. It can be a very painful and challenging thing to do and of course there are some people that are better at handling this fact than others. If you ask anyone what they think about their own mortality you will get a wide range of answers, varying from the extreme that they can't mentally process or accept that one day they will eventually cease to exist from the world and at the other end of the extreme are those that live in constant fear that one day they will die. And of course many of us go back and forth between these two extremes, depending on life situations.

The issue becomes when looking at these two extremes, is that the person that can't fathom their final day of existence, might not truly comprehend that they have a finite amount of time and thus essentially waste it on trivial things. Contrary to the person that is in constant fear of death, will be impaired by that exact same fear and hamper their ability to truly live their lives because they know that one day they will perish from the world. I believe that if we can take these two extremes and face our fear of death, in which one that makes sense to us if we dissect them, such as we do have a limited time here on earth and thus we must not waste it on things that are unimportant to us. Instead it simplifies our overall purpose as a result of the limited time we have here and that is to follow our heart and focus on the things that bring us happiness such as our relationships and enabling whatever life you can, so that it too can attain its highest development.

This is why we must constantly seek the edges of our lives, because in essence, we have a limited time. We must continually grow so as to get to know our world as much as we can and help life move along with the utmost will to live. Seek the ways in which you can positively help the unraveling and development of life in the universe, but start within yourself. We learn in two different ways – by understanding or by feeling something emotionally/physically. This is why, for most of us, this universal purpose is forgotten, and thus we fail to continue seeking our own growth. In our daily lives, it becomes impossible to sit and ponder this predicament we have with the universal purpose and our societally instilled purpose. Since we can't feel this universal concept in the same manner that we, say, feel the warmth of the invisible rays of the sun, or feel the love of a mother, we can choose to approach it by understanding it instead.

How can we become better at enabling life in the world while we are here? By understanding that all life deep down seeks growth and enrichment. Thus, by engaging in this very action, it makes us more capable of helping enrich the world around us. The higher we grow, the further we can see and understand our very own existence in the universe, which allows us to have a greater positive impact during our time here, as we fulfill our higher purposes.

Fertile Soil

Just like plants need fertile soil to grow, so do we. It's very difficult for a plant to emerge from a seedling if the right conditions are not met. A plant needs nutritious soil through which it can take in the nutrients required for it to propagate. This is the same case for us.

We have to seek a certain environment which invites and promotes growth in our lives. Many times, we are in a certain place in which our growth is oppressed or even completely looked down upon, like a dark blanket being thrown over us so that we can't absorb the light. Sometimes, we are like a plant that is trying to grow in toxic soil. It becomes very hard or even impossible to grow in these kinds of environments, regardless of how much we want to grow. Sometimes it is our very own friends or even our families that impede us from seeking true growth, but in many instances, it's also our very own choices and our reliance on willpower that keeps us from growth. Pause for a moment and think about your current environment. Take a piece of paper and draw a small stick figure of yourself in the middle, with one arrow pointing up and the other down. At the top end, make a list of the people and things that pull you up towards positive growth, such as your mentors, friends, teachers, family, and most importantly, your dreams/heart's calling/reasons for seeking growth. On the bottom end, list all the people and factors that pull you down or impede your growth, such as certain places where you tend to go, your fears, your inhibitions, vices, negative people around you who are envious of seeing others grow or succeed, people who are only concerned with what benefits them, or people who don't seem to act with their hearts.

If we are in arid soil and want to grow, we must seek to set the right conditions for our own growth. We can't depend on the world or others to do this for us, as there are times where we can't just wait for the rain and sunshine to come. If you are currently in an environment where it's dry, dark, and cold, where growth becomes extremely difficult, build yourself your own greenhouse and set the conditions you need to grow. You cannot let the world set your limit for growth. Look at your list and seek to eliminate the people and environments which affect your growth negatively, and look towards the factors that promote it.

Sometimes, this can be one of the hardest things we can do in our lives. We are so used to living in a certain environment that it becomes scary to leave the environment that we have lived in for so long. This can entail losing friends, having people talk bad about you, changing your belief system that you have known to be true all your life, changing your routines, or sometimes even feeling completely alone, but that's what we must do if we want to truly seek growth.

This is not a scorched earth method, though, in which you eliminate everyone from your life just because you're seeking change. We are all interconnected and need each other to grow as a whole. Therefore, spend your time around people who are constantly uplifting you, and who seek to help you reach your potential. Anybody who is seeking true growth wants to see others grow as well, and thus, having one friend like this is better than having a hundred friends who prefer to see you below them, as they are afraid you will cast a shadow over them and take in all the light, when in reality we can all bask in the light of universal life. As you start doing this, you will attract more and more people who are on the same wavelength as you are. You no longer need to have a greenhouse, where you have to control your own environment, because you will eventually see yourself growing in a bright, green, fertile field, where everything around is encouraging you to grow.

Part Six- Unity and Friendship: The Keys To Our Survival

"What I'm not confused about is the world needing much more love, no hate, no prejudice, no bigotry, and more unity, peace and understanding. Period."
—Stevie Wonder

I searched the words "universal unity" on google to see what would come up. I was curious to see what the thoughts on universal unity were, or if there was even such a term. Most of the results that came out talked about unity in religious or political institutions. For example, every religion strives to unite the very people that are believers of that faith. Although, the overall end result of this goal has unfortunately at times been a division of society. The symbols on a church show its belief, boundaries on a map have put imaginary walls between the very people we live with, and the difference in languages has made it often times difficult to communicate. The color of our skin, the clothes we wear, the jobs we do, the places in which we live, and the amount of money in our bank accounts have all instilled a kind of false difference between us. I believe that universal unity is the realization that we are all interconnected and that we live within nature, versus believing that we and nature are two completely different entities. The Edge of Universal unity is the ultimate understanding of the synergy we have between the universe and ourselves. The more we strive to understand this, the closer we will be to our hearts. When we follow this edge, it sets us onto a path of greater understanding in many aspects of our lives.

Universal unity, in our world today, I feel has been broken down into many different labels. What religion are you? What language do you speak? Where do you work? Where do you live? How much money do you make? As a result, it has caused a distortion on how we view ourselves and others. On a large scale this has separated us from the realization of belonging to one world and inherently sharing the world with those around us. The lights of the city have made it difficult to see the stars that surround our planet, which serve as a reminder that we in a way are very dependent on each other. By looking at earth in terms of the universe itself, we eventually become part of this living organism, therefore everything on earth is interdependent of everything else that coexist inside of it. How we pollute one river in a city, impacts the next cities that it runs through which then impacts the ocean in which that river drains to, then impacts the rest of the ocean and its life. The realization that our actions affect the whole is a notion that has been difficult to fathom. We become so preoccupied with our lives that it makes it incredibly difficult at times to think that our everyday actions impacts the world around us. And yes! It is really hard to think about this all the time. I feel though that if we can think about our lives and become cognizant that our actions affects our surrounding environment, the way in which we deal with the world around us might change a bit. This is beautifully explained by Paramahansa Yoganda as he says-

"Millions of people never analyze themselves. Mentally they are mechanical products of the factory of their environment, preoccupied with breakfast, lunch, and dinner, working and sleeping, and going here and there to be entertained. They don't know what or why they are seeking, nor why they never realize complete happiness and lasting satisfaction. By evading self-analysis, people go on being robots, conditioned by their environment. True self-analysis is the greatest art of progress".

I believe we all long for closeness with each other and our hearts. We are in constant desperation to find this. We often times do jobs based on how much they will pay us, we go to colleges based on what popularity they have, and we become friends with others because of our commonalities and interests. We were born with universal unity etched into our hearts. As we grow up in society, this universal unity starts to get diced up and split up into all the categories of things that, in a way, connect us all despite our differences. There's so much information flooding our brains today that, in a way, this unity that we're supposed to have with the world around us has been blurred.

Google CEO Eric Schmidt stated that "Every two days now, we create as much information as we did from the dawn of civilization up until 2003". That is incredible, compared to even 50 years ago. On a daily basis, we are exposed to so much information, whether that's what happened on the morning news, who posted what on Facebook, which of the hundred shades of blue we are going to paint our bedroom walls, or what we are going to wear to a restaurant. Our minds have been so overloaded with information that they're constantly having to analyze these things and make choices on them. Where is the time to focus on your heart and give your energy to others, when it is being spent just trying to get through the day? It's like being at a rock concert and trying to have a conversation with someone.

We must not forget ourselves and become blurred visions to the people around us. We all desire the same basic elemental things. As stated earlier, Abraham Maslow, determined that all humans have five core needs which we instinctually seek. In order of importance, they are: Physiological, Safety, Social, Self Esteem, and Self-actualization. The ways we seek them might vary, but at the end of the day, we are in some way striving to fulfill each of these needs. The stuff in between is what divides us. Each of us is at different levels of fulfillment, and as we seek to fulfill our needs, we tend to forget that everyone else – regardless of race, sex, color, ethnicity, or ability – is also seeking the same basic needs to sustain their lives.

Butterfly Effect in Us

The Butterfly Effect is a term coined by Edward Lorenz, in which he explains that one single event – no matter how small – changes the course of the universe forever. Every single action we do today impacts those around us forever.

We must try to remember this as we go through our lives with the friendships we develop, the strangers who we meet, and the people who we love. We are all products of each other's interactions towards each other. Some of us build each other up and some of us tear each other down. You might not think of this, but a couple of words or even a small gesture can actually change someone's life, a hundred-fold. We might not know how our words affect others, but we should strive to be conscious that it's constantly happening around us. It's hard to fathom that a genuine smile and a gesture of appreciation can literally set someone's day in motion, but they can.

When we look at nature, we can see that even the most minute fish or rain drop is important. When one species disappears, it can cause the disturbance of an eco-system. The collection of raindrops become streams, and the streams join together to create rivers. The amount of water we use directly affects the health of the planet and ourselves. It's a constant cycle of action and reaction. It's hard to look at the world in this manner. It's so immense that we can't feel the connectedness between all the things on the earth, let alone the universe. This is something that is extremely hard to feel, but we can seek to understand. We impact the world around us whether we know it or not. Just like all the natural processes in nature create a synergistic interaction between each other that affects the earth as a whole, we too are part of that process. We tend to see ourselves as apart from the natural world, as if we are not part of that collective synergy that makes up our world and the tiny speck of space of the universe we take up.

What I want you to realize is that you do play an important role in the direction of the world. Just like the drops of the rain coming together to form the rivers, our actions collectively add up to set the course of our humanity today. We live in a world where we are constantly plagued by society to conform, so that it becomes hard to see how our small actions affect the world as a whole. Thus we should listen to the wise words of the great emperor Marcus Aurelius as he says *"What we do now echoes in eternity"*. The actions we take now essentially ripple throughout time and it is our choice for that ripple to affect the world around us either positively or negatively. This is true for both nature and ourselves. By understanding this, we start to see that we are all extremely powerful beings, and that every single one of us is important and plays a part as humanity strives to push our world forward.

Magnetic Field of Our Hearts

There was a great experiment done to explain how each one of us has the power to change the frequency of the world through our hearts. It's has been scientifically explained that our hearts produce a measurable magnetic field. It's hard to believe because we can't see it, but we can somehow feel it. This magnetic field fluctuates depending on how we are feeling, and just like atoms affect each other when they interact, depending on their level of energy, we too affect each other's magnetic field. This is explained by physics and magnetic fluctuations in our hearts. We are part of the natural world and we work under the same physical principles that all things in the universe operate under. Our bodies have electricity, and the fluctuations in electricity during heart palpitations create a magnetic field. Here is a quick abstract explanation of this physical phenomenon from a scientific article:

"Although in physiology the heart is often referred to as a simple piston pump, there are in fact two additional features that are integral to cardiac physiology and function. First, the heart as it contracts in systole, also rotates and produces torsion due to the structure of the myocardium. Second, the heart produces a significant electromagnetic field with each contraction due to the coordinated depolarization of myocytes producing a current flow. Unlike the electrocardiogram, the magnetic field is not limited to volume conduction and extends outside the body. The therapeutic potential for interaction of this cardioelectromagnetic field both within and outside the body is largely unexplored." –Excerpt from Med Hypotheses. 2005;64(6):1109-16.Cardiac torsion and electromagnetic fields: the cardiac bioinformation hypothesis. –Pub Med

What we know about electric currents is that they can be affected by magnetic forces, thus we are all constantly projecting a magnetic field around our hearts, and we are actually affecting the electric currents or people's hearts, thus affecting their brain, since our brains also create a magnetic force (significantly smaller than that of our hearts). One can see the constant interaction between these two generating forces – our hearts and our minds. They are in perpetual interaction with each other. There have been studies done in which the heart's ECG from a newborn actually syncs with the mother's brain EEG (used to measure brain activity), and to her ECG rhythm (used to measure heart rhythm). The study noted here theorized that this allows the mother to be more aware of or in tune with her baby. She can feel him/her and understand him/her better. This is such a complex method that this interaction has not yet been fully explained by science. The scientific community does agree, though, that we generate a magnetic force, and that magnetic forces affect electrical currents which in turn affect our magnetic forces.

The Global Coherence Institute, or GCI, which is comprised of people from all around the world, has been studying the magnetic field of the earth since 1998 to see if there are any fluctuations in the earth's magnetic field. They do this by measuring the resonant frequencies of the plasma waves that circle the earth's ionosphere. The purpose behind this study is to answer this question: if our hearts and minds generate a magnetic force, is it powerful enough to affect the earth's magnetic field? Even though the study is still ongoing, the institute has seen deviations happen during particular world events such as 9/11 and President Obama's inauguration.

"When human consciousness becomes coherent, the behavior of random systems may change. Random number generators (RNGs) based on quantum tunneling produce completely unpredictable sequences of zeroes and ones. But when a great event synchronizes the feelings of millions of people, our network of RNGs becomes subtly structured. We calculate one in a trillion odds that the effect is due to chance. The evidence suggests an emerging noosphere or the unifying field of consciousness described by sages in all cultures." –Global Conscious Project

The Institute of Heartmath has performed numerous studies in brain to heart interactions and how they affect our consciousness and perception of ourselves, as well as how they affect the world around us. From this research, they came up with the term "coherence" to describe the state of emotions in comparison to the spectrum analysis radiated by the heart's magnetic field. They have concluded that when we feel different emotions, this causes changes in the spectrum analysis of the heart's magnetic field. Therefore, our emotions are translated to the heart and the heart translates them to the world around us in the form of a magnetic field which can affect others around us.

Coherence is when the heart and the mind are synergistically intertwined, cases in which you are guided by both your mind and your heart. When this happens, we immerse ourselves in a flow-like state. These are the times in which we begin to walk to the edges of our lives. This is what many athletes explain as 'being in the zone'. I believe that it is during these times when we are closest to our hearts. These are the times when all your inhibitions no longer matter, and you act as if nobody is watching. These are the moments that you act with full trust in yourself and your heart.

If we simply just look at the science, one cannot disagree with the fact that our hearts and mind generate an electromagnetic force, and that magnetic forces can affect electrical frequencies (generated by our hearts and minds). When you measure a brain's EEG, you are in fact measuring differences in electrical charges which, when combined, depict the current brain frequency. If this happens, then we must also be able to be affected by others' magnetic generated forces, but is this happening all the time and how do we know we are being affected by it? As explained by Gregg Braden:

"Our brains generate an electrical and a magnetic field, but they're relatively weak, as compared to the heart. The electrical field of the heart is about 100 times stronger than that of the brain, and the heart's magnetic field is about 5,000 times stronger than the magnetic field of the brain. Our own physics textbooks say that if you want to change the atoms of physical matter, you have to change either the electrical field or the magnetic field; the heart does both."

I want to open you up to the possibility that the way in which we see the world can impact those around us, whether we understand it or not. By acknowledging this, we then begin to be more conscious of ourselves and our hearts. We become more aware of the potential power we have within ourselves, and the true abilities we possess to affect the world around us for the better. This makes us all connected in the form of magnetic interactions, as magnetic lines run infinitely, just their strength decreasing exponentially in relation to the distance.

These are very hard concepts to imagine, as it is hard to believe the connectedness and power we all share between each other and nature. It's incredibly difficult to believe in what we can't see, yet often times we can feel and measure this. When we look at the physics in play and natural examples all around us, we have to agree that the same concepts apply to us, also. The greater the disconnect that happens between us and nature, our ability to get into this coherence state between mind and heart lessens. We no longer become guided by our hearts, but instead are driven by society's acceptance of a certain standard.

Travel and Understanding

The Edge of unity is one where we feel and understand that essentially every living thing in the world is in synergy with each living organism and each living thing is given the chance to exist in the universe. Every seed, every newborn, is given that spark-like jolt in which darkness all of sudden opens to light as the seedling cracks open, or the newborn first opens his eyes to see his/her mother's face. We all have been in complete darkness, and all of a sudden, the curtains open and this wonderful world appears in front of us. We are all born in this exact same way. Who or what makes this occur? Who gets chosen? Maybe nobody picks? This is why I believe that every single one of us is good, and has the universal purpose etched in our hearts. It is when we lose this sense of unity that we begin to act against the natural world and each other.

I'm from two very different countries. I was born in Venezuela in a small southern ranching town called Barinas, and then moved to the United States around the age of nine. I remember being young and watching the Disney club in Venezuela, and thinking, " I'm never going to go see Disney World" and basically seemed like a dream. Little did I know that it was soon going to happen. As you leave your country of birth for good and move to the U.S you are literally given an alien number. You essentially become an alien in that country. If you look up the definition of "alien" on the Webster dictionary it defines the word alien as: *not familiar or unlike other things you have known, different from what you are used to, from another country, too different from something to acceptable or suitable.* When you move to a different country, you get to see a side of humanity that not everyone gets to see. I was able to experience the longing and sadness that comes with being an immigrant. At the age of eighteen I could count on my hand the number of times that I was able to see my father after I came to the U.S. You experience the great disconnect that happens between family as you no longer see them often. It's like pages out of your life have been ripped out. There is a great adjustment period that comes with it also, forgetting your old friends and sometimes your culture. Life, in a way, begins anew.

The great lesson I took from this experience is that, even though we all live in different places around the world, we all long for a spirit of unity between each other. We might eat different things, speak differently, and have different skin colors or appearances, yet we all desire the same basic things. Imagine that you can be born into any part of the world, and grow up there. We don't have a choice about what area of the world we are born into. This is what's senseless about racism and the way in which people have enslaved other human beings. Some people believed slavery was ok and that it was the "natural order" of the world, were being guided by previous societal beliefs, instead of being guided by their hearts. Even though there were many people who were being guided by their hearts such as Thomas Jefferson who understood that slavery was actually a terrible crime towards humanity and this unity we all share. Yet today we face the similar struggle of what society vs what deep down our hearts believe is right. If we got closer to this Edge of unity and closer to our hearts, many of the negative societal beliefs would be overwritten.

We have to expose ourselves and accept all cultures in order to get closer to this Edge of unity. Remember, as you seek your edges, you will begin to get closer to your heart. We begin to feel the Edges of compassion and gratitude as we meet others who might not have much in terms of monetary wealth, yet still have enormous hearts. We have to open ourselves to these experiences, because the more we do, the easier it is to hear our own hearts and understand the unity we all possess.

Instead of focusing on acquiring more unneeded material things, focus instead on getting closer and experiencing the world around you. It's hard to understand this concept of unity if you remain in a bubble and remain in the comfort of your defined boundaries of people or places. This doesn't mean you have to get into a plane and fly to a different country right away. What I mean is that instead of saving up for that new TV or cell phone, try to instead spending less on material things and spend more of it on traveling. In the meantime though one can simply start by going hiking in nature or welcoming those who might be different from us culturally.

If you are able to travel to other places and experience different cultures though, it can get you closer to the Edge of unity as you become more accepting of others that are different from you culturally. When we travel, we learn. Instead of reading a book about a place, we are hearing it, seeing it, smelling it, touching it, and feeling it. The more worldly experiences we have, the easier it is to get closer to our hearts and humanity. Which in turn makes us realize that we are all on the same journey, and must remain steadfast in the bond we all have with each other.

We Are All Wanderers

Have you ever wondered what drives us every day? Regardless of what we are doing, there is something unique about us if we look at the very thing that drives us all. If we look back at our ancestors, we can't even begin to wonder how much we have transcended the past and moved on into the world that we have today. From caves to houses, from the first rock wheels to the formula one cars we have today, from the few story-tellers around a fire to the incredible availability of knowledge about the world which we have on the internet. How did this all come about? What is the significance of this journey?

When we look at history books, there are always periods where you look at the reason why there was a conflict or problems where humanity had to face, and we can't help but ask, what were they doing? How come they didn't know how to solve that specific situation or problem? They were all on a journey of reasoning and understanding; in other words, they were all on a journey to find the significance of the world around them. It's like humanity has been going on this never-ending journey of finding the new. We're on a journey of touching, feeling, tasting, and experimenting, and along the way, we make mistakes. We are all addicted explorers of the world and our lives. We are all on this same journey. We have all been wandering through the world with this need to explore what lies in the future. This is the human condition that brings us all together.

The early cavemen, the pharaohs of Egypt, the Aztec Indians, and the Native Americans are all like every single other human out there, past or present, as well as each other. We have the spirit of searching the present to find what lies in the future.

In this search for reasoning and understanding, we also have developed the advancements we see today. The core driver, though, is a spiritual, naturally infused push to seek understanding of the mystical world we live in. This is the difference-maker in humanity today, and why we have been able to advance technologically. We all long for what new experiences life will bring to us. Our future husbands and wives, our future jobs, our future places we will see, our future children and grandchildren.... Life is constantly giving us gifts and new experiences as we search for them. It is a kind of universal law, one where nobody should be allowed to suppress or deny this right to anyone else.

This is a kind of unity which some of us have forgotten. We are literally in this together. The one thing we truly know today is that earth is the only planet that safely harbors life and yet we wonder how truly significant that is. We keep exploring to push the envelope of this meaning. Life is such a mystical gift that it's even hard to fathom or accept. Immense amounts of money are spent in seeking new planets for existence, as if we have almost given up on the very thing that allowed us to be born into this universe. The place where it took an estimated 4.5 billion years for the conditions to be just right, in order for our existence to be permitted.

I believe in space exploration, as I think it provides us with more and more evidence of how inimitable our planet is. Space exploration has shown us the barren planet of Mars, the icy landscape of Pluto, and the vastness of it all. Yet, this serves to give our existence and our planet significantly greater meaning which I believe we all seek. It makes our trivial problems significantly less important, and in essence brings us closer together. Therefore, we must help the world around us achieve this continuation of longing to explore the present, to find the new. We are all facilitators of this, and therefore should serve as encouragement for others to seek the world around them.

The moment we decide to stop exploring and wandering, or begin inhibiting another's journeys, life stops developing. You get in the way of the natural course of life. Don't ever lose your sense of wonder and exploration. You are never too young or too old. Join the world in its search for reasoning and understanding of the magnificence that our existence in the world really is.

One Makes a Difference

In a world that is filled with constant distractions and noise, it's very difficult to lead ourselves by our hearts, and instead we are led by trends/limitations that are put on us by society. Too often, we accept the norm even though that norm might not be right. We accept things based on the capacity that is allowed to us by the naysayers. There are always going to be those people who, in fear of them not being able to do it themselves, put their fears on others as if to make themselves feel better. None of them want to be proven wrong. There are plenty of those people in our world today, who are afraid of the human endeavor and what the human race may be capable of. We know these people hide in many corners of our lives, and they too are in fear of the unknown. They are afraid of getting close to their edges, as what they will feel might scare them along the way. This is what makes someone a great leader, as they take on the burdens and fears of others, or others' inabilities to face their fears of the unknown or of hard work, in order to get close and feel the edges of life.

As we accept this, we must rise up and start our journeys towards the edges, to combat the naysayers and show the world the path towards the Edges of love, courage, action, growth, and unity. The current beat of society is being led away from these edges, and into the dark forest. The fog tries to engulf us and get us to lose our headings. We all face these conditions at different levels. There are those who have very little power, but as they become united, their power is then based on their numbers. The world is full of entitlement without work, with achievement and little effort, with control and disrespect, with fear and acceptance of the inhuman. Always remember that fact, and always push towards the advancement of the natural life.

We have to be the beacon for society because we cannot simply sit here and wait for someone to decide to pick up the torch and lead us in the direction of our edges. We must take it upon ourselves to analyze our edges of life which must be sought in order to maintain our deep reverence for our existence in the world today. We must be the example for others to follow, and ignite the numb and the fearful. We have to serve as examples for others who are moving away from the edges, thus, accepting comfort and vanity in order to fit in to society. The people that stand against our world, for the greedy acquirement of monetary wealth or power, have to be defeated. The reason they are able to have power is because the people around them have allowed it to be so. These people have distanced themselves so far from their hearts and the edges that would otherwise enrich them spiritually, emotionally, and mentally. It becomes a sort of give and take, as we walk away from the edges toward which our hearts call us to go. Regardless of where you are in life, you can always begin to move towards these edges and be a positive beacon for humanity.

Final Part- Till Death Do Us Apart

"When your time comes to die, be not like those whose hearts are filled with fear of death, so that when their time comes they weep and pray for a little more time to live their lives over again in a different way. Sing your death song, and die like a hero going home."--Tecumseh

Death can be a difficult subject to talk about. All of us fear death, so we often tiptoe around our lives to avoid any reminders of it. It's difficult to feel this feeling that we are no longer going to exist. It's hard to fathom life without ourselves, yet we know that, just as we are born into this world dedicated to the preservation of life, our lives will eventually cease. Our memories will be held by the ones we love, and eventually after some time has passed, we will be eventually forgotten.

Most of us subconsciously live our lives understanding this, which creates a sort of fearful view towards the world. We fear the ceasing of our life here, thus keeping us from opening our hearts towards the beauty of the world. In a way, this creates a sort of desperate approach to life. John Lennon said:*"There are two basic motivating forces: Fear and love. When we are afraid, we pull back from life. When we are in love, we open to all that life has to offer with passion, excitement and acceptance. We need to learn to love ourselves first, in all our glory and imperfections. If we cannot love ourselves, we cannot fully open to our ability to love others and our potential to create. Evolution and all hopes for a better world rest in the fearlessness and open-hearted vision of people who embrace life."*

We must shift our view of death, as one that brings the end of our journey here. Instead we must look at death as something that encourages and gives importance to every single living thing on earth. It also serves to lessen the egotistical importance we give ourselves and solidify the fact that it is not the world that owes us something, but that instead, we owe something to the world.

What We All Share

When we hear the word 'death', it automatically brings sadness and fear for most people. There's a negative connotation to what death brings, which is completely acceptable. The news and horrific events in the world have somewhat shaped what death means to us, and has instilled the fear of it in our minds. Our understanding of death varies in all of us as those who have lost a loved one, have a greater understanding of it versus someone who hasn't. We grieve when our loved ones die. After they pass, the only thing that is truly left is the memories we have of them and the impact they had on us, and on the world. Death is a part of life that in a way gives significance to it, and bonds us all together.

Many of us tend to forget that death is eventually part of life. In order to live more passionate lives, we need to walk closer to the Edge of death and understand it. We must understand that life needs death in order for it to have value. Death is the equalizer to all things, regardless of how much power or wealth you have accumulated; death doesn't discriminate. As we look at life this way, it opens up our hearts a bit more. It makes our time here extremely precious. You have the opportunity to be here for a short period of time and then, after a while, your time here will end, and all that will be left behind in eternity is the people you touched, and the love you left behind.

This approach to death makes the trivial problems of our lives less important. The egoism starts to melt away and our approaches to our lives become more meaningful. The realization that we have a set amount of time in this world, where, when the lights go out, the person we were and the body we occupied will cease. What would you want to leave behind for those coming after you? What gifts do you want to leave behind for your children, or give back to represent the legacy of those who worked hard to leave us with a better world before they left it, so that we could enjoy it ourselves? To the millions of soldiers around the world that have given their lives for their countries so that their children could enjoy a better world. This gives us all immense significance in how important each and every one us is to our very own existence. The representation of our world is calculated by the addition of every single one of our actions, regardless of their being big or small.

I believe that, if we all knew our exact time of death, we would all live more purposeful lives. It has become a kind of illusion that our lives will eventually cease. It's something that is hard to feel and understand. Therefore, many of us live our lives saying, "I'll just do it tomorrow, I'll just make it up tomorrow, I'll love more tomorrow, I'll be healthier tomorrow, I'll think about my dreams tomorrow", or "I'll destroy the natural world, so that I can be rich today, and let the next generation fix it". It's a constant vicious cycle that many of us get into, thinking we'll have more time, and the next thing we know, we are in our death beds weeping and praying that we had more time.

We are all bonded by the fact that we all have a limited time in the world. Death is an extremely sad event that represents the passing of life, but most importantly, it gives life significance as our time here becomes precious. We therefore must look at each other and realize that our existence is highly dependent on those who came before us. We must always seek to reach our potential as our time here is extremely special. We should not be scared by the thought of our lives ending, or the thought that the world has no meaning because life eventually ends. We should use this realization to push us forward and unfreeze us from this fear of the end.

One of my favorite explanations of why we should push for our edges and reach the limits of our potential is beautifully explained by the bestselling author Marianne Williamson's book, *A Return To Love*: *"Our deepest fear is not that we are inadequate. Our deepest fear is that we are powerful beyond measure. It is our light, not our darkness that most frightens us. We ask ourselves, Who am I to be brilliant, gorgeous, talented, and fabulous? Actually, who are you not to be? You are a child of God. Your playing small does not serve the world. There is nothing enlightened about shrinking so that other people will not feel insecure around you. We are all meant to shine, as children do. We were born to make manifest the glory of God that is within us. It is not just in some of us; it is in everyone and as we let our own light shine, we unconsciously give others permission to do the same. As we are liberated from our own fear, our presence automatically liberates others."*

Feel The Edges

Use death as a means of understanding the world around you and the purpose you serve within it all. The torch of life has been handed down for thousands of years to us now, coming from those before us. We are all carriers of this torch as it is a given right when we are born, and we pass it on as we die. Remember how important you are in the grand scheme of all things. In this specific moment of time, you are carrying the most vital element to life in the universe – consciousness. Do not get lost in the trivialities of life, by living a life constantly searching for entertainment and distractions to keep your mind busy and away from the real significance you represent to the world. Do not let the torch that has been passed, by those who no longer exist, slip away, as there are those in the world who seek to put it out. We all share this important purpose within our hearts. We are meant to love the world around us and seek our innermost selves by seeking the edges of life and following our hearts.

You Are Life

There's a great story told by the famous Japanese monk, Yoshida Kenkō, where he tells the story of a man who is buried in a graveyard. From his apartment window, he can see the marked grave. He describes the sad event as the man's family members being all around him, crying and deeply saddened. After that, his family members continue to visit the grave, and then after several years have passed, rarely does anybody visit the grave, and after a while, the grass and vines start growing around the marked stone. Kenkō explains that after the man's family passed away, his memory died with them. After several more years, the tomb started to be overtaken by nature, to the point where people could barely see what was written there, and after several more years, the marked stone was eventually taken over by nature, and the crumbled rock buried under the sweeping soil and dead leaves. He depicts the whole ordeal as the man and the tomb, coming full circle and going back to nature.

This concept and understanding has reverberated throughout history, as in the King James Bible, Genesis 3:19, " *In the sweat of thy face shalt thou eat bread, till thou return unto the ground; for out of it wast thou taken: for dust thou art, and unto dust shalt thou return*". This part *"till thou return unto the ground"*, there is a basic assumption and understanding

135

of our mortality. It is an acceptance of death as a natural part of life as we were made from the dust (elements), and when we die, we essentially return back to dust. Regardless of whether you are religious or not, this statement speaks volumes, as it was written about fifteen hundred years ago. This is a historical account of the understanding people had back then.

We must accept this basic understanding of death as it is simply a part of life. We have to come to terms with death in order to value life. We live in a society where our cows, pigs, and chickens appear to us in a prepared fancy package for us to cook. Graveyards that used to be located next to churches have been hidden away in the outskirts of our towns, and death and tragedy have become the hyper focus of news reporting, so much that we have become numb to it as we watch and eat our dinners. We have greatly separated ourselves from the concept of death, so much that we have in essence lost touch with the importance and meaning of living. Our regard for life has diminished in many of us, as we get distracted by the noise around us.

The knowledge we can take from the natural world is that the natural world, such as the plants and animals, don't exist with the purpose of diminishing the world around them, but enriching it for the next generation of life that follows them. All living things are in constant co-existence with each other, and essentially, each one needs the other to thrive. Plants produce oxygen so we can breathe and water quenches our thirst and thus they allow for the existence of life.

The living processes of life are in constant evolution to enrich life and keep it going. It is a constant cooperation between all the things in the natural world to sustain that which is life. Yet, many of us have forgotten our parts in this synergy of the natural world. Some of us have become numb and complacent to the meaning and the part that we play on earth. Things like greed, gluttony, laziness, envy, ignorance, and materialism have blurred our natural purpose or course in the world. It has disturbed our minds and has darkened the edges of our lives. Many of us have deviated from this natural divine purpose that the universe has set forth. We must understand that our time here is very meaningful and beautiful, and as Carl Sagan said

"Some part of our being knows this is where we came from. We long to return and we can. Because the cosmos is also within us, we're made of star stuff. We are a way for the cosmos to know itself" therefore from the dust of the stars that we were created to dust shall we one day return.

Reaching Understanding

As the ancient philosopher Lao-Tzu once said, *"if there is to be peace in the world, there must be peace in the nations, if there is to be peace in the nations, then there must be peace in the cities, if there is to be peace in the cities, there must be peace between neighbors, if there is to be peace between neighbors, there must be peace in the home, if there is to be peace in the home, then there must be peace in the heart."* Any change that you seek in the world starts with you. Our hearts have a constant longing to be in order with this natural universal purpose. When this message is silenced by the distractions of our daily lives, we feel a sense of discomfort, a sort of calling that we can often hear, yet can't understand.

Complacency or insufficiency have distorted this message. Complacency has brought on inaction and insufficiency has produced greed. They have disconnected us from what truly matters, and our ultimate purpose. The purpose to reach our full potential by constantly seeking the edges that enrich life, and working to become better suited to help sustain/develop it. When we start seeking these edges in ourselves, they bring greater understanding and joy into our lives. They push us to what Physicist Michio Kaku says is a type 1 civilization. A civilization that is planetary, where a whole civilization works together for the common goal of sustaining all life on earth, which then allows us to be interplanetary and secure our existence.

He states we are in type 0 civilization, but we are currently in transition to a type 1. For example, such as English being the 2nd language most commonly known, or the uniting of European countries who in the last thousand years have had consistent conflicts and war with each other, they have formed the European union and coming together for a common cause of existence. All over the world, people are rising up against corruption and inequality. The invention of the internet being a kind of world phone through which everyone can connect with each other.

We are moving towards our Edge of unity, but most importantly of all, we are in a very important time of human existence. It is imperative to move towards this type 1 civilization of greater understanding of the role we all play in securing the future for those that follow or one day we will cease to exist, and yet the universe will continue. We are either walking towards our edges and listening to our hearts, or walking in the noise of the world around us, away from our edges. This is what we must constantly have in mind as we sit and analyze our lives.

Just like before death, as you lie there and are close to the end of your journey here on earth, all your inhibitions, worries, fears, and vulnerabilities begin to strip away. All of a sudden, it's the core you present, and one realizes that his/her time is of great significance to the natural world. How much did you love? How many times did you stand up against fear? How many lives did you touch in a positive way? And most importantly of all, how did you leave the world in the places through which you walked? Your time here becomes enormously meaningful and important. This thought of one getting ready to end one's journey in the world is a very disconsolate thought, but it teaches us to learn to experience these moments now in our lives, and not wait till the end.

Remember your importance in the world, yet remain humble to the magnificent opportunity and task you have been given in the universe. When you are given the opportunity to be born into this world, you can never forget your natural purpose in the universe and the important role you play in it. I feel this in those moments when I'm in awe of a majestic landscape or experiencing a special moment in which my breath pauses for a second. That's when I can feel my heart, as the noise quiets momentarily. I feel it when I step out into the ocean and can experience the sight, smell, and sound of ocean waves. It serves as a reminder that everything around me is alive. The ocean waves beat in a kind of frequency where, as each wave crashes, it's as if you can hear the earth breathing. These are the times that think about the bigger picture. The petty problems in our everyday lives lose meaning, our greed is forgotten, and our hearts are opened.

Begin now to seek those edges in your life that bring you closer to your heart. Don't follow the crowd, follow your heart. Do those things in your heart which enrich/sustain life around you, and most importantly, remember it starts with you. Don't be afraid to think about your death. Use that understanding to fuel your courage, spark your action, and help you remain humble as you walk the world. Don't be afraid to seek your Edges of love, courage, action, and growth. Don't let these be your only edges. Search for those which your heart seeks, and those that give you a greater understanding of the world around you. As you continually seek them, the noise of the world will quiet as you steadfastly carry life to the next generation. Always have an insatiable hunger to do those things which fill your heart with joy and feed your soul. Forgive yourself from the past and begin to walk towards your edges.